THE TIMES TRAVEL LIBRARY
Edited by Paul Zach

Published in India in 1989 by
Time Books International
25-A, Khan Market, New Delhi 110 003

© Times Editions 1989
1 New Industrial Road,
Singapore 1953

Printed by Tien Wah Press, Singapore
Colour separation by Far East Offset, Kuala Lumpur
Typeset by Superskill Graphics, Singapore

Cover: Visitors to the Taj Mahal form an interesting
contrast to the mausoleum's white marble backdrop. They
come from all over India adding a touch of vigor to the
scene.

Endpapers: Dawn at Agra is a spectacle to behold, as
the golden orb of the sun casts a haunting silhouette of
the Taj Mahal.

Frontispiece: India dons all its varied and colorful
finery in a grand parade along Raj Path against the
backdrop of Rashtrapati Bhavan, the Presidential
Palace, on Republic Day in New Delhi. Perhaps no
other city in India reflects better the country's sharp
contrasts.

ISBN: 81-85113-19-X

DELHI · AGRA
FATEHPUR SIKRI

Photographs by
Raghu Rai and Nitin Rai

Text by
Lai Kwok Kin

Designed by Leonard Lueras

Time Books International
New Delhi

This page: The calm waters of the Yamuna River mirrors the splendor of the Taj Mahal, which as a monument built for a loved one, has inspired poets and writers for over three centuries.

Following pages: The Salim Chishti mosque in Fatehpur Sikri, dedicated to the priest who blessed the emperor Akbar with a son; rides on elephants and ferris wheels during a fair in Agra bring joy to children, most of whom are descendants of the Mughals who built the city and erected the Taj Mahal; a mother with her young child watches spellbound as a hot-air balloon rises over a large, open field in Delhi; Muslim devotees prepare for prayer by washing themselves at a long pool in front of the Taj Mahal. The Mughals devised intricate water channel systems in their gardens to keep themselves cool during the searing heat of north Indian summers.

Contents

Delhi, Agra and Fatehpur Sikri

Where Worlds Collide

Dawn breaks in Old Delhi. The sun's rays are golden, outstretched fingers that peel back the night to reveal a barefoot worshiper kneeling in the courtyard of Jama Masjid, India's largest mosque. Its loudspeakers blare out the muezzin's call to prayer and shatter the morning calm.

Soon the rest of Shahjahanabad, as this ancient Mughal city is called, will awake, shake off the languor of the north Indian summer night and fill its streets with a frenzy of activity. Men, women and children wend their way past the throng of horse carts, goats and cows in the warren of bazaars and alleys hidden among centuries-old monuments.

A short ride away, the tinted glass panes of cardboard skyscrapers glisten above Connaught Circus, a circular row of Georgian-style, two-storied buildings. Young executives in well-pressed shirts and ladies in saris of stunning colors stride briskly to their air-conditioned offices in the commercial hub of the new city. As dusk falls, they step into their nippy Japanese Marutis and maneuver into the traffic. They pass emaciated waifs begging at intersections and zoom into the tinsel world of Delhi's five-star hotels.

India is a land of sharp contrasts and it is perhaps in Delhi that one becomes most acutely conscious of this. Two worlds in one city, two worlds that meet but refuse to surrender their past entirely to the present. Delhi strains against the shackles of its past as it hurtles toward the 21st century, trailing in its wake an ancient civilization that now accounts for a sixth of mankind.

Flanked by the Aravalli ridge on the east and the Yamuna river on the west, the capital of India is growing fast, some say too fast. When Prime Minister Jawaharlal Nehru proclaimed India an independent nation in 1947, New Delhi was home to half-a-million people. The city's population is now passing the 8 million mark and will touch 12 million by the turn of the century.

Calcutta, the former capital, has fallen into decay and Bombay is bursting at its seams. But New Delhi's industrial juggernaut is rolling outwards across the north Indian plains, gobbling up virtually all the available land in its path. It is no longer

merely the bureaucratic capital of India dependent on the commercial lifeline of other ports. New Delhi has become a metropolis in its own right, drawing planeloads from all corners of the globe. The expanding industries act as a magnet to masses of people who pour in from surrounding states in search of a better life.

Such is the pace of expansion that many older Delhiites are beginning to wonder if the city is losing its soul. But Delhi has a soul. It's just that it is caught in limbo between its past and its future. You can

Only when seen from the air can one truly appreciate the size of India's biggest mosque, Jama Masjid, and its massive courtyard (left). Thousands still gather every day for prayers at the mosque which was completed in 1656 by Shah Jahan (above).

15

scarcely drive 10 minutes in the city without seeing an ancient monument or ruin. A dome here, a crumbling wall there.

And then suddenly, as if from nowhere, there looms some majestic edifice such as Humayun's tomb or the massive Presidential Palace built by the British. Each little corner presents something new, rewarding the interested observer with another piece

the grand vision of ruling Hindustan from Delhi. The city's strategic importance in north India was unchallenged.

The British gained effective control of the country after the Indian Mutiny of 1857 and in 1915 set about building New Delhi. The capital of India, the brightest jewel in the crown of the British Empire, was "in every way to be worthy of this ancient and

to fit into this amazing jigsaw. Many *Delhiwallahs* themselves will admit that their city's history is too complicated for them to grasp.

The roots of this intriguing city stretch back beyond 2,000 B.C. when it was first mentioned in Hindu and Jain texts. From the 13th century five Muslim dynasties made it their home even before the dramatic advent of the Mughals in 1526. By the time the British arrived in the 19th century, seven cities had already flourished on the site. For all their differences, the sultans and the British were similarly captivated by

The Republic Day parade, held every January 26, commemorates the declaration of India as a republic in 1950. Here an Indian airforce fighter jet glides past the two-kilometer expanse of Raj Path in a display of India's military might.

beautiful city." What they created was more than worthy of the old. Designed by Sir Edwin Lutyens, it is redolent of the splendor of the Raj and a moving testament to the blend of classical Western and Indian architecture. In 1931, the British completed the grand city with its parks and wide, tree-lined avenues leading up to the impressive Viceregal Palace. But they spent only 16 years glorying in their capital before a newly independent India claimed Delhi as its own.

For all the architectural contributions of the British, the credit for transforming the cityscapes in the plains of north India goes largely to the magnificent Mughals, a race of rulers at once ruthless and artistic. The Mughals swept from the west across the Indian plains to claim the subcontinent of

Hindustan and then turned their attention to architecture with equal zeal. One emperor in particular was noted more for his architectural endeavours than his martial success — the extravagantly romantic Shah Jahan.

Driven by grief at the death of his wife, he constructed the Taj Mahal, an inspired monument to the power of love. He spent millions of rupees and 22 years building this

Archaeological finds in the 1950s and 1960s of artifacts dating to 1,000 B.C. suggest that Delhi may well be the site of Indraprashta — the abode of Indra, Lord of the Firmament — described in the Hindu epic, the Mahabharata. But other excavations reveal only that the settlement was definitely occupied from the 3rd century BC during the Mauryan period. In 1966,

stunning marble tomb in Agra. It now stands in the eyes of the world as a great wonder and a symbol of India itself.

Agra, a sleepy village 203 kilometers south of Delhi, remained unremarkable until the great Mughal emperor Akbar decided to transform it into his capital. Razing old buildings, he replaced them with the massive Red Fort, completing it in just eight years. For a brief period, he transferred his capital to Fatehpur Sikri, a palace-city he built in gratitude to a Muslim priest there whose blessing brought him a son. Lack of water forced him to return and rule from Agra. The Mughal capital shifted back to Delhi during the reign of Shah Jahan, and Agra lost its pride of place. But because of the Taj Mahal the city never faded completely into obscurity.

to the delight of archaeologists, an inscription of the 3rd century BC Mauryan emperor Ashoka was found on a rock outcrop in the Aravalli hills near the present-day city.

Myth and fact mingle to form the ancient lore of Delhi. The origin of the name is uncertain. Historians say it could have come from the Hindi word *Delhali* or the Persian word *Dehleez*. Both words mean threshold and, indeed, Delhi was the gateway to Hindustan.

In the 10th century AD, the Rajput ruler Anangpal planted the seed of the site's first

The old and new meet in Delhi to celebrate Republic Day. A spectacular panorama of marching bands and traditional folk dancers (above) parade in an hour-long procession along Delhi's central vista watched by thousands of celebrants.

17

real city of Lal Kot, near Qutb Minar in southeast Delhi. It was left to one of the Chauhan kings who succeeded him, Rai Pithora, also known as Prithviraj, to enlarge Lal Kot and rename it Qila Rai Pithora. Prithviraj successfully fought off the invading Turk, Mohammad Ghori, in 1191 but was defeated in a second encounter which cost him his head. Thus began one of the most turbulent periods of Delhi's history.

Ghori installed his slave, Qutb-ud-Din Aibak, who established the Slave Dynasty in 1206. It was the first of the Delhi sultanates. Qutb-ud-Din tore down 27 Hindu or Jain temples to build a giant mosque and the Qutb Minar minaret, which towers over modern-day Delhi.

The line of sultans that followed lasted to 1526 when the Mughals overrode the Afghan ruler, Ibrahim Lodi. Each of the next dynasties — Khalji, Tughlaq, Sayyid and Lodi — contributed monuments and settlements of their own to Delhi's rich but confusing history. Between them they left six cities. The last was Purana Qila, near the present-day Delhi Zoo, erected by the Afghan invader Sher Shah Suri who temporarily ousted the Mughal ruler Humayun in the mid-16th century. The styles of architecture they left add a variety of Islamic influences to a dominant Persian theme.

In 1526, at a time when the Lodi dynasty was in chaos, the Mughal buccaneer Babur marched from Kabul in present-day Afghanistan across the Khyber Pass with 12,000 men. He defeated Sultan Ibrahim and sent his son Humayun off to secure the treasure of Agra. Three days later, he marched into Delhi. That marked the start of the Mughal empire, an era which would change the face of the city as much of India. It would also leave a legacy of Muslim architecture unparalleled in scope and refinement. The Mughals, who used Delhi and Agra alternately as their capital, left an indelible imprint on both cities.

After Babur's death in 1530, Humayun sat uneasily on his father's throne. He laid the foundation stone in 1533 for a new city

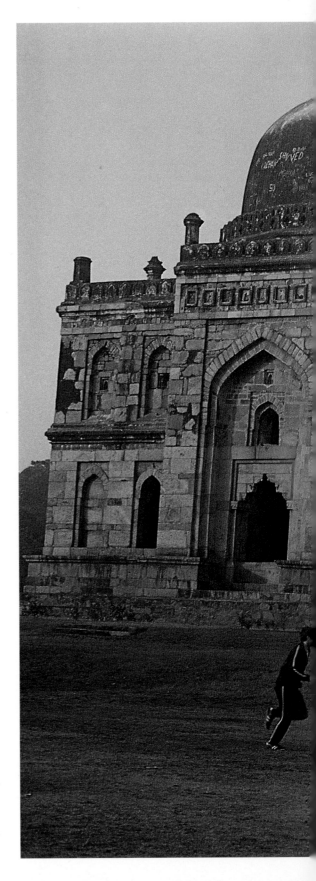

It is difficult to travel far in Delhi without stumbling across ancient ruins such as this monument in the sprawling lawns of Lodi Gardens, which contain the tombs of the Lodi kings. Of Afhan origin the Lodis were the last ruling family of the Delhi sultanate.

called Dinpanah (Asylum of Faith). But his plans were interrupted by internal strife and the invasion of the Afghan Sher Shah Suri. He defeated the Mughal army and forced Humayun to flee across the Yamuna River on an inflated animal skin.

Sher Shah Suri built many roads as well as much of the sixth city of Delhi, known as Purana Qila. Humayun improved upon the

city when he regained the empire in 1555, nearly 16 years after he had lost it. But his return to power was to last only a few months. In 1556, while descending the steps of his library, he slipped and fractured his skull. He died three days later. A dim period of Mughal history passed away with him.

Ironically, one of the finest monuments in Delhi is Humayun's tomb. It was built by his senior widow, Bega Begum, nine years after his death. The mausoleum south of Purana Qila is considered the first substantial example of Mughal architecture.

Mughal architecture has left the strongest imprint in Delhi. The characteristic domes and red sandstone structures can be seen in the ruins near Qutb Minar (above) and through the main gate of Humayun's Tomb (right).

Mahatma Gandhi leading thousands in the famous Dandi Salt March in 1930 to protest against the Salt Tax by the British rulers is immortalized in this giant statue in New Delhi. Gandhi is revered as the father of modern India.

Historical Chronology

The Ancients

BC 1000 — Painted Grey Ware pottery discovered in 1955 at the site of Purana Qila in east Delhi suggests that Delhi was the site of Indraprastha, or the "abode of Indra," Lord of the Firmament, as described in the great Hindu epic, the Mahabharata.

BC 300 — The rise of the Maurya Dynasty. In 1966, an inscription of the Maurya emperor Ashoka (BC 273-236) was discovered engraved on a rock outcrop near Srinivaspuri in the vicinity of Delhi.

The Rajput Period (900-1200)

circa 900 — Surajpal of the Tomar clan of the Rajputs builds Suraj Kund, an amphitheater-pool south of Delhi. Anangpal, another ruler of the same dynasty, builds Lal Kot, said to be the first city of Delhi. In 933, permanent occupation of Delhi begins.

circa 1160 — King Vigraharaja IV of the Chauhan dynasty (also Rajput) captures Delhi from the Tomar Rajputs. His grandson Prithviraj III, also known as Rai Pithora, extends Lal Kot and names the enlarged city Qila Rai Pithora.

1192 — Prithviraj dies while fighting Muhammed of Ghor, an invader from the Afghan hills, who retired to his native land leaving his slave Qutb-ud-Din Aibak as viceroy to India. Qutb-ud-Din starts building the Quwwatu'I-Islam mosque by demolishing 27 Hindu and Jain temples in Lal Kot.

1193 — Qutb-ud-Din captures Delhi, which was then still in the hands of the Chauhans.

1199 — Qutb-ud-Din lays the foundations of the Qutb Minar, probably as a tower of victory or as a *"minar"* to call the faithful to prayer. It would later be completed by his son-in-law and successor Iltutmish (1211-1236).

The Delhi Sultanate (1206-1526)

1206 — Qutb-ud-Din enthrones himself at Lahore as the first sultan of Delhi and starts the Slave Dynasty.

1265 — Ulugh Khan Balban, a slave of the last sultan in Qutb-ud-Din's line, declares himself sultan.

1290 — Feroz Shah, a Turk of the Khalji tribe in the Delhi court, captures the throne from Shamsud-Din Kaimurth, the last king in Balban's line, and assumes the title of Ala-ud-Din. He founds the Khalji dynasty, extends his reign and captures the fortress of Chittor despite the fierce defense of the Rajputs. Delhi, for the first time, becomes the capital city of India.

1303 — Ala-ud-Din lays the foundation of the second city of Delhi, Siri, a few kilometers northeast of Lal Kot. He also digs the vast reservoir at Hauz Khas.

1321 — Ghiyas-ud-Din Tughlaq, a Turk nobleman, leads a revolt and is proclaimed king. He founds the Tughlaq dynasty, the third in the Delhi Sultanate, and starts building Tughlaqabad, the third city of Delhi.

1325 — His son, Muhammad bin Tughlaq, comes to power and builds Jahanpanah, the fourth city, between Lal Kot and Siri.

1351 — Feroz Shah Tughlaq, Mohammad's nephew, builds Ferozabad, the fifth city, on the western banks of the Yamuna River.

1398 — Timur the Lame charges down from Kabul and defeats an army of elephants at Panipat before taking Delhi, but he chooses not to stay and returns to Samarkand with 120 elephants and many of Delhi's craftsmen and stonemasons.

1413 — The 11th and last of the Tughlaqs dies.

1414 — Khizar Khan ascends the throne, founding the Sayyid dynasty, the fourth of the Delhi Sultanates.

1451 — Buhlul Lodi, an Afghan, captures the throne and starts the Lodi Dynasty, the last of the Delhi Sultanates. Sikander, the second ruler in the dynasty, shifts his capital to the vicinity of Agra and builds a new city called Sikanderabad.

The Mughal Dynasty (1526-1857)

1526 — Babur invades Hindustan with his army of 12,000, sweeping down from the west to defeat Ibrahim Lodi at the battle of Panipat. He takes Delhi and Agra and founds the Mughal Dynasty.

1540 — Babur dies having conquered much of India but not entirely consolidating his territories. His son, Humayun, takes over. Humayun starts work on Purana Qila, the sixth city, around 1540, but is ousted from his throne by Sher Shah Suri, an Afghan who had once served Babur. Sher Shah completes much of Purana Qila before Humayun wrests back the throne in 1555.

1556 — Akbar is enthroned at the age of 14 after Humayun falls to his death from the library steps at Purana Qila. Akbar goes on to rule as the greatest Mughal emperor until his death in

1605. He chose Agra as his capital.

1565 — Akbar starts building the Red Fort at Agra. It is completed eight years later at a cost of Rs 3.5 million.

1569 — Akbar begins work on Fatehpur Sikri.

1574 — Akbar completes Fatehpur Sikri and the capital is moved there from Agra.

1584 — The court returns to Agra, apparently because of the shortage of water in Fatehpur Sikri. Akbar starts building his tomb in Sikandra, where he is later buried. He is succeeded by Jahangir, who rules from 1605-1627, and Shah Jahan, ruler from 1627-1658.

1600 — England's Queen Elizabeth I grants a trading charter to the East India Company.

1632-1654 — Shah Jahan builds the Taj Mahal.

1638 — Shah Jahan transfers the capital from Agra to Delhi and lays the foundation for Shahjahanabad, the seventh city. He also begins work in 1639 on Lal Qila, the Red Fort.

1648 — Shah Jahan completes Shahjahanabad.

1658 — Aurangzeb, the last of the great Mughal rulers, deposes his father Shah Jahan.

1659 — Aurangzeb is crowned in Delhi after gaining victory over his other brothers. Shah Jahan is imprisoned in the Agra Fort and looks out across the Yamuna at the Taj Mahal until his death in 1666.

1707 — Aurangzeb dies. The Mughal empire goes into a period of decline.

1739 — Nadir Shah, a Persian ruler, invades Delhi. He initiates an orgy of killing in Shahjahanabad before returning to Persia with the Peacock Throne.

1857 — Indian **Mutiny** breaks out. Muslim Sepoys, claiming that pig fat was used in the cartridges, revolt against their employers in the East India Company. The British quell rebellion and exact revenge in Delhi. Bahadur Shah, the last Mughal emperor, is exiled to Burma.

The British Raj (1858-1947)

1858 — The crown imposes direct rule over India.

1876 — Queen Victoria is proclaimed Empress of India.

1911 — December 12, King George V announces at Delhi Durbar that the capital of British India will be transferred from Calcutta to Delhi.

1920 — Indian **nationalists** begin the Non-Cooperation Movement.

1930 — Mahatma Gandhi leads the famous Dandi Salt March to protest against the Salt Tax.

1931 — New Delhi is formally inaugurated the capital of India.

Independence (1948-Present)

1947 — India gains its independence from Britain on August 15.

1948 — Mahatma Gandhi is assassinated on January 30.

1950 — The Constitution of India comes into force on January 26.

1966 — Indira Gandhi becomes the first woman prime minister of India.

1977 — Indira Gandhi is defeated in national elections.

1980 — Indira Gandhi is returned to power.

1984 — About 1,000 people die when the Indian army storms the Golden Temple in Amritsar, the holiest Sikh shrine. On October 31, Indira Gandhi is assassinated by her Sikh bodyguards. That unleashes a backlash by Hindus that leaves more than 2,700 Sikhs dead in riots in Delhi in the first three days of November.

1984 — Indira's son, Rajiv Gandhi, is sworn in as Prime Minister and wins a general election in December.

Trees sprout from the ruins of Fatehpur Sikri, which was abandoned soon after completion due to a lack of water. Nearby stands the Hiran Minar, a tower with numerous elephant tusks protruding from its walls, which the emperor Akbar erected in memory of his favorite elephant.

The use of high arches, double dome and square garden were later to reach their pinnacle in the design of the Taj Mahal.

Humayun's death gave the stage to the greatest Mughal ruler, Akbar (1556-1605). The brilliant soldier-king chose to make his capital in Agra where he built the massive fort. A brand new city at Fatehpur Sikri served as a home for only 15 years. He

returned to Agra until his death in 1605.

Delhi remained relatively in the Mughal backwaters until the reign of Shah Jahan (1627-1658). This greatest of Mughal builders erected the Taj Mahal in Agra. With work still in progress, however, he shifted his capital back to Delhi in 1638. Shah Jahan began building the massive Lal Qila, the Red Fort, in 1639 on the banks of the Yamuna. He also laid the foundation for Shahjahanabad, the seventh city completed in 1648.

Another of his creations was the mammoth Jama Masjid mosque completed in

A magician performs tricks for tourists behind Delhi's Red Fort (above). Built by Shah Jahan in the mid-17th century, over a six-year period, the Fort is so called because of its red sandstone walls. Today it is a major tourist attraction.

1656. It remains one of the biggest mosques in Asia today. His wives and daughters would later build mosques, tombs, and a canal through Shahjahanabad

The reign of Shah Jahan marked the zenith of the Mughal Empire. The elegance and luxury of Shah Jahan's court was unmatched. Inside the walls of Lal Qila, the court was alive with music and dance performed while fine food was served. Foreign dignitaries were received in the Diwan-i-Am (Hall of Public Audiences) where Shah Jahan sat on a marble throne inlaid with semi-precious stones. In the Diwan-i-Khas (Hall of Private Audiences), under a ceiling ornamented with silver, was the fabled Peacock Throne made of pure gold and inlaid with diamonds, rubies and sapphires. The throne cost nine million rupees and seven years' work. Both in Agra and Delhi, the marble inlay work was at its finest during the time of Shah Jahan. Walls were adorned with precious and semi-precious stones. A complex and intriguing chain of fountains and special water channels ran through the gardens and buildings alike, keeping them cool even at the height of summer when it is very hot.

The luxurious life within the walls of the fort are neatly described in an inscription in the Diwan-i-Khas:

If on earth there is paradise
It is this, it is this, it is this.

Shahjahanabad, built around the fort and enclosed by a 6.4-kilometer stone wall, was

Workers pause by the roadside to eat their lunch of *chappati* and *dal* (unleavened bread and lentils). Only late at night does the city lapse into sleep. Entire families huddle on pavements, swathed in dusty blankets. It is a part of Delhi which the casual visitor often misses. It is the heart of the city.

A walk through Chandni Chowk is an

at its liveliest during this period. Streets were jammed with traders from neighboring countries, advertising their wares at the top of their voices in the center of the bazaar. A canal with a tank in the middle of this bazaar glistened on moonlit nights, giving it the name Chandni Chowk — Moonlit Square.

Three hundred years later, the walled city, though considered the more derelict half of Delhi, still bristles with smells and cacophony. Autorickshaws, nasty three-wheel contraptions that sputter exhaust and noise, jostle for space with hordes of humanity. Muslim women clad head to toe in traditional chador cloaks stop occasionally to make a purchase from vendors sitting on the roadside, their anthills. of groundnuts heated by a smoky dung fire.

endless voyage of discovery. Half a dozen ancient wooden box cameras stand outside a Jain temple waiting for patrons seeking instant black-and-white passport photographs. A vendor pumps refrigerated water from a huge box set on a tricycle. In the brutal heat of Indian summers, business is brisk at a half-rupee for a glass of water or one rupee for a delicious concoction of rose syrup and lime juice.

Children trying to earn a living stand on the pavements hawking aquarium fish in old whisky bottles. Two youths operate a giant wooden cane crusher next to a

*Life goes on under the shadow of famous monuments in India. Here, beside the abandoned city of Fatehpur Sikri, village life continues as it has done for centuries (**above**). The settlement of Sikri was built by Akbar in 1570 to commemorate the birth of his son Jahangir.*

grubby-fingered *pan-wallah* who wraps betel nut in leaves.

Turning off into Dariba Kalan, a row of silver shops offer a vast array of old and new ornaments and artifacts. Dozens of silversmiths and jewellers huddle by small lamps working with tools and in methods virtually unchanged for three centuries. Octogenarian shop owners clutching tiny

nances which alienated the Hindu population. In 1675, in front of a large crowd in Chandni Chowk, he beheaded the Sikh guru Tegh Bahadur. The Sis Ganj temple now marks the execution site. Aurangzeb died in 1707 at the age of 89. The Mughal dynasty had controlled much of India for 181 years under six great rulers. Now its best days were behind it.

brass weighing scales haggle with a customer beneath a glass display filled with necklaces, jewel boxes and bangles of every conceivable design.

But Old Delhi as it stands today is only a shadow of its former glory. It started to crumble not long after its builder Shah Jahan fell ill in 1657. His son Aurangzeb (1658-1707) imprisoned him and then murdered another brother to proclaim himself emperor of Hindustan.

Life in the city was never the same again. Aurangzeb ruled with an iron hand for half a century. He issued strict Muslim ordi-

Much of India's ancient customs remains intact today. Cows pull an altar during a procession to celebrate Lord Krishna's birthday in Old Delhi (above). A shopkeeper in Agra welcomes customers under the watchful gaze of dozens (right).

Aurangzeb's son, Bahadur Shah (1707-1712), stepped into the Mughal throne at the ripe age of 63. He lasted only five years, mostly spent struggling to keep the empire from disintegrating. The Sikhs, Jats, Rajputs, and Marathas all rose in revolt, with the latter making incursions into Delhi itself. For all their squabbling, none of the Mughal rulers lasted more than a few years on the Peacock Throne.

Then in 1739 the Persian invader Nadir Shah marched into Delhi. Riots broke out, and 900 Persians died. In retaliation Nadir Shah ordered his troops to butcher more than 30,000 people in one day as he watched from the roof of a mosque. The Mughal emperor, Mohammad Shah, begged Nadir Shah to end the massacre, saying, "If you want to continue the killing,

*Rain or shine, visitors trek daily through the magnificent gardens surrounding the Taj Mahal to behold India's most famous monument (**above**). Tourists are the lifeline of Agra, snapping up postcards or souvenirs such as alabaster miniatures of the monument, and of the builder and his beloved (**left**).*

then put the life back into those you have destroyed for none now remain." Shah stopped the carnage. But he stayed only long enough to cart home the Peacock Throne as well as the Koh-i-Noor ("Mountain of Light") diamond.

In 1803, emperor Shah Alam, frustrated by invasions which nibbled at the Mughal Empire, asked for assistance from the British who helped quell a rebellion by the Marathas. The Mughals came under British protection and for the next 50 years, Delhi was a tranquil place.

The fragile peace was shattered on May 11, 1857 when native soldiers of the East India Company mutinied in nearby Meerut. What caused it is uncertain. Theories vary from the alleged use of pig or cow fat to grease new cartridges — which offended Muslim and Hindu soldiers respectively — to aggravation over the dismissal of local rulers. The mutiny spread across India and helped sow the seeds of Indian independence. It also gave the British government an excuse to assert their authority and rule and go on ruling the country for 90 years.

The Sepoys, who left their barracks in Meerut, met up in Delhi, and proclaimed the 82-year-old Bahadur Shah emperor. The British, backed by Sikh soldiers, breached the city wall and retook Delhi fort after a fierce battle. Cannon and bullet marks can still be seen at Kashmir Gate and Lahore Gate.

Bahadur Shah fled with his family to Humayun's tomb, where two of his sons and a

grandson were seized by Major Hodson and shot on the way back to the fort. Bahadur Shah was exiled to Burma, bringing three centuries of Mughal rule to an ignominious close.

The British exacted their pound of flesh after the mutiny. Hundreds were hanged for their part in the revolt and bazaars around Chandni Chowk were razed. Terrified men cut the throats of their wives before committing suicide, rather than be executed.

A contemporary author, Michael Edwardes, wrote:

A giant cement sundial built in 1724 by the astronomer-king Raja Jai Singh II intrigues a group of boys in New Delhi (left), while younger children busy themselves with less academic pursuits in another part of the city under the shadow of skyscrapers (right).

Perhaps the most revolting aspect of the violence was that the executioners seemed to enjoy what they were doing. Within a few days of the capture of the city, the provost marshal officially hanged between four and five hundred, and it was said on good authority that the soldiers had bribed the executioners "to keep them a long time hanging, as they like to see the criminals dance a 'Pandies' hornpipe, as they termed the dying struggles of the wretches." When a great multiple gallows was erected in the city, "English officers used to sit by it, puffing at their cigars, and look on at the convulsive struggles of their victims."

In the months following the mutiny, Delhi's population shrunk from about 200,000 to 60,000 and the city wore a desolate look. Homes were empty and the bazaars deserted. British soldiers and Sikhs fighting for the British army had plundered the city before the government appointed agents to stem the looting. The scene was reminiscent of sackings by Nadir Shah and other Muslim invaders through the ages.

Members of the Mughal court and harem were turned out from the palace. Many ended up as prostitutes or street entertainers around Chandni Chowk. The British

*Like its more famous sister, the Ganges, the Yamuna River is also regarded as sacred by Hindus. Relatives weep at a funeral along the Yamuna in Delhi (**left**) while further along the banks, corpses await cremation before the ashes are scattered on the river (**above**).*

Place of Victory

Just 38 kilometers from Agra rises the shell of an almost-perfect palace city. Fatehpur Sikri is a capital city built to honor a Muslim saint who blessed Emperor Akbar with his first son. It takes its name — the Place of Victory — from Akbar's conquest of a neighboring state.

Today Fatehpur Sikri stands as a remarkably well-preserved palace city. There's good reason for that. It has hardly been lived in. Akbar abandoned it soon after it was finished, probably because it was lacking in fresh water.

Akbar was crowned at age 14 after the sudden death of his father Humayun. He grew up to become a great emperor, a master at war and skilled at riding elephants, playing polo and hunting. His only setback was that at the age of 26 he had still failed to sire a son and heir among his many wives.

In 1568, Akbar stopped in Sikri, once a Rajput village. He sought blessings from Sheikh Salim Chishti, a particularly religious priest who made regular visits to Mecca on pilgrimage caravans.

The saint was confident of his own blessings and Akbar's virility. He promised the emperor that he would have not one but three sons. And he did. The delighted Akbar founded a city on that very spot. When his Hindu wife bore his first son a year later, he promptly named him Salim and set to work immediately to build his capital city of red sandstone there.

The boy grew up to become Emperor Jahangir. Jahangir tells a strange story about the old priest. Akbar had asked when the saint would die. Salim pointed to the infant Jahangir and said that when the young prince recited something from memory, the priest would depart to "the abiding region."

Akbar immediately issued strict orders that young Jahangir was not to be taught recitation. But when Jahangir was nearly three, an old maidservant apparently forgot the rule and taught the little prince a couplet. He went to Salim and repeated it. As he had predicted, the priest fell ill that very night and died soon after.

Akbar erected a sandstone mausolem for the priest which was later covered with white marble by Jahangir. Today women seeking blessings for a child still come to the mausoleum. They tie a red string on the perforated screen and promise to return for a second visit if their wish comes true.

Akbar was a shirtsleeves emperor. He helped quarry and transport the red sandstone to the new capital himself. The city was well-connected to Agra by road. Much of it was erected by 1570 and Akbar moved his court there in 1574.

The early English traveler Ralph Fitch described Fatehpur as "greater than Agra, but the houses and streetes be not so faire." He said Akbar had 1,000 elephants, 30,000 horses, 1,400 tame deer, 800 concubines and such a store of leopards, tigers, buffaloes, cocks and hawks in Agra and Fatehpur "that it is very strange to see."

Akbar oversaw most of the construction. It bears his distinctly simple style and shows unique innovations and motifs incorporating various religious influences.

It was in Fatehpur, a city that at one time measured 11 kilometers in circumference, that Akbar spent his happiest days. He perfected his administrative skills, introduced land revenue collection and developed a new religion called Deen Ilahi. The religion combined elements of Hinduism, Buddhism, Christianity and Islam, but failed to catch on.

In the evenings, after handling the affairs of state and debating religion, Akbar would climb the five-story Panch Mahal, an open-air wind tower. There he would relax and watch the ladies of the court play "pacheesi," a game like chess in which the women dressed in costumes moved in a large courtyard carved with designs like a chessboard. It formed the basis for the popular western board game, Parcheesi.

He would then retire to his Khilwatkada-i-kas and have the same ladies brought to his room through a hidden passageway. Later he would be lulled to sleep by music played below by his favorite musician Tan Sen.

For all its glory, Fatehpur fell mysteriously into obscurity and decay in 1854 when Akbar moved back to Agra after having lived in the new city for only 14 years. Historians generally believe that he vacated the court because it lacked fresh water.

Fatehpur relived some of it former glory, however, when Jahangir sought refuge there for three months in 1619 to escape a plague that swept Agra. But invading Jats sacked Fatehpur at the end of the 17th century. Thereafter it fell to ruin until the turn of the 20th century when the Viceroy, Lord Curzon, decided to restore it. Today the Archaeological Survey of India is still carrying out excavations which may eventually shed more light on Fatehpur's ancient secrets and glories.

As dusk gathers, a man contemplates the darkening scene from the walls of Fatehpur Sikri near Agra. This city of red sandstone, built by Akbar in 1570, is one of the most perfectly-preserved Mughal palace cities today.

erected army barracks in the Red Fort, ugly structures which mar the stately palace to this day.

But order was soon restored. Calcutta continued as the British capital, but the importance of Delhi was increasing. The first train rolled into the city in 1867. Ten years later, before a Durbar gathering of anyone who was anyone, Victoria was proclaimed Empress of India by the Viceroy, Lord Lytton. A second major Durbar, attended by British rulers and maharajahs resplendent in their traditional finery, was held in 1903 by Lord Curzon to celebrate the coronation of Edward VII.

On August 25, 1911, Lord Hardinge took the decision to make Delhi the capital of British India, sending a secret note to the Secretary of State. He argued that the masses in India still regarded Delhi as the capital. He said moving the capital from Calcutta to Delhi would "strike the imagination of the people as nothing else could, would send a wave of enthusiasm throughout the country and would be accepted by all as the assertion of an unfaltering determination to maintain British rule in India." The decision was announced in the third Delhi Durbar on December 12, 1911, by King George V himself.

Once made public, work began briskly on the mammoth project. The city was completed in 1931 at a cost of 15 million pounds. The "eighth city," which would reflect the glory of the British empire and accommodate 70,000 people, was designed by Sir Edwin Lutyens and his assistant, Herbert Baker. More than 30,000 unskilled workers were hired and an unimaginable 700 million bricks were used.

But construction was marred by a series of mishaps, blunders and disputes. King George V and Queen Mary laid the foundation stone but planners later chose an alternative site for the Viceregal Palace. Lord Hardinge, riding an elephant, was injured in a bomb attack while inaugurating the new city on December 23, 1912. Lutyens and Baker were locked in a perpetual dispute

A sea of turbans, big and small, parade in New Delhi on Republic Day. This auspicious day is celebrated by Indians from all walks of life and from different communities. A polyglot land, India has a colorful and rewardingly rich cultural heritage.

41

One of New Delhi's most spectacular structures, Humayun's Tomb (**left**) is an architectural precursor of the Taj Mahal. Another impressive monument is India Gate (**below**) built in 1931 to honor 60,000 Indians who died in World War I.

A Tale of Two Builders

New Delhi was built from scratch by the British rulers during India's colonial period. But it was designed and planned by two men whose working relationship was marked by mutual dislike. Their constant battle of wits exasperated and tickled their superiors at the same time.

Chief architect Sir Edwin Lutyens was noted for his genius in Western classical styles. The British appointed him to provide an overall plan for the city and design the grand Viceregal Palace (now Rashtrapati Bhavan) and India Gate. He was assisted by Herbert Baker, who was to design the two secretariats and Parliament House. Lutyens had befriended Baker in his student days.

The two men immediately crossed swords over the question of what elevation the palace should be built at. Lutyens insisted it should be built at a higher level than the two secretariats housing the civil service. He argued that the palace should be built on the highest point of Raisina Hill so that it would stand out when viewed from the great square below.

But Baker wanted the secretariats to share the hilltop with the palace. That way both Viceroy and his bureaucrats would be on the same level, forming a united whole that would reflect the notion of democracy.

Baker won the dispute. His superior had to move his pet project back to accommodate the secretariats which now flank the palace.

Lutyens then realized that the steep road between the secretariats blocked the view of the palace from the great square below. For six years he fought the battle of the gradient. But it was a losing battle. Baker also won round two.

Baker was more adept with the workings of the bureaucracy. He successfully held on to the Government Court, an open ground between the two secretariats. This, combined with the high cost of altering the incline of the hill, blocked Lutyen's efforts. He had met his "Bakerloo," he remarked. The two men stopped speaking to each other.

Lutyens never forgot the incident. Later, he did manage to exact revenge over Baker's design of Parliament House. Baker had proposed a structure with a high central dome rising from the base with three wings spreading outward to accommodate three council chambers. Lutyens denounced it as too elaborate, saying neither "God nor Michaelangelo" could make sense of it.

Instead, Lutyens proposed a circular design. Baker grudgingly accepted. The giant Parliament House as it now stands has been criticized as looking like a gasometer and bullring. Baker himself called it a merry-go-round.

Despite the acrimonious relationship, the two men completed their task. New Delhi was formally inaugurated in January 1931. But not before Lutyens fought and won battles with other more formidable opponents.

In the early 1910s when plans for the city were first made, Lord Hardinge, who was then viceroy, felt strongly that the main buildings should be in traditional Indian or Mughal style. The king agreed with him.

Lutyens disagreed. He said, "Personally I do not believe there is any real Indian architecture of any great tradition."

Begrudgingly, Lutyens adapted some Indian features, though, such as the latticed window and the umbrella dome. He sought to win support for his ideas from the vicereine, Lady Hardinge, using his native wit.

Once, he was questioned for disobeying her instructions. He offered to make amends by washing her feet with his tears and drying them with his hair. "It is true that I have very little hair, but then you have such very little feet," he said.

Lady Hardinge promptly forgave him.

over the final shape of the city and its buildings. The first World War also interrupted work for several years.

When the new city was finally inaugurated in 1931, its scope, breadth and beauty was startling. Roughly hexagonal, the focus of the city was Connaught Place — whose concentric rows of colonnaded shops were to be the city's commercial heart — and the magnificent Viceregal Palace made of red sandstone.

Later renamed Rashtrapati Bhavan, or Presidential Palace, the three-story Viceregal Palace is set in 15 acres of gardens. Within the gardens are a swimming pool, eight tennis courts, cricket grounds and a nine-hole golf course. At the height of the empire, 2,000 people were employed by the Viceroy and the Palace was home to 6,000,

including families and dependants.

But the pomp and grandeur fizzled out at midnight of August 14, 1947 when Prime Minister Jawaharlal Nehru stood on the ramparts of the Red Fort and declared India independent.

Under its new leaders, New Delhi has developed a unique Indian-ness. While turning into a modern metropolis, it remains very much at heart a city of bureaucracy and politics. It is here, in the countless government offices that the cream of India's civil service — a briefcase brigade

*Spring in Delhi breathes life again after the winter cold and transforms a nursery into a riot of colour (**above**), while a group of farmers (**right**) harvest cauliflower on the outskirts of the city to be sold as produce for the market.*

Riding the Maharajahs' Train

The splendor and opulence of the era of the fabled maharajahs is recreated aboard the Palace on Wheels, India's version of the Orient Express and Asia's most expensive train ride. It rumbles across north India's hot and dusty windswept plains every week, making whistle-stops at embattled forts and palaces in Rajasthan that have been turned into luxury hotels.

For kingly prices of US$800 to $1,500, tourists in search of the old, forgotten glory get to wine and dine on the vintage trains. Once they were used by former princes who were renowned for their excessive wealth, unusual sense of styles and sometimes bizarre tastes.

The 20 wooden coaches include two restaurant cars and a bar saloon. All were resurrected from scrapyards, museums and storerooms and put into service by the Indian government. The oldest coach dates back to 1898. It was built on the order of the maharajah of Bikaner.

The steam-hauled train has been all but phased out in the west with the advent of diesel engines. But India is one of the few countries where steam engines are still in active use. Nostalgic train fanatics often leap onto the engineer's car, help with shoveling coal and tug at the whistle chain to warn off the occasional wild camel before jumping off at the next station.

For others the ride is probably the most convenient way to see half a dozen Rajasthan forts, with the Taj Mahal in Agra and the nearby Bharatpur Bird Sanctuary thrown in as a bonus. It eliminates the bother of checking in and out of hotels and hassling with taxis and tour guides.

The rail tour begins and ends in Delhi. It operates only between the cooler months of October and March and covers a breathtaking 2,600 kilometers (1,600 miles) of stunning views of sunrise and sunset in the Thar Desert.

The indulgent maharajahs were permitted to build their own trains by the British rulers. But they allowed them only to be run on a one meter (3 foot, 3 inch) gauge track instead of the standard 4 foot, 8 inch gauge. That helped prevent the Indian rulers from quickly ferrying large bodies of troops that could prove a threat to the Raj.

On board, the settings attempt to transport passengers back to the days of majestic lifestyles. Ever-smiling attendants in blue tunics and flowing red turbans wait on guests hand and foot by day. At night they roll up the silken bedspreads. Their exquisite service has been hailed by discerning passengers. And a fat tip is expected at journey's end. But not all is comfort and opulence, however. Veteran train-riders complain that they rarely go away feeling like a prince despite the best efforts of the staff.

It's not surprising that the company has had trouble getting out of the red-ink in its accounts. The finishings, food and facilities on board are not as pristine as the Orient Express. They are in dire need of improvement. The pace of life on board can also border on the hectic.

Palace on Wheelers (perhaps appropriately known for short as POWs) are often rushed from fort to tourist emporium with scarcely time to relax. From the first stop's "Welcome Palace on Wheels" banner, passengers are garlanded, then herded on board caparisoned elephants or camels and rushed back to the train at day's end.

Back on board the train, which sports a dull yellow coat of paint, modern-day maharajahs often have to play musical chairs. They take their meals in shifts in the tiny restaurant cars. Beds are exactly six feet long and prove a problem for many Caucasians, while toilet seats are smaller than normal.

Alas, the past glory of the maharajahs is something even money can't buy.

Train lovers with cash to spare relive the grandeur of kings on board the Palace of Wheels. Liveried waiters pour drinks in the elegant bar of polished teak on board the train which was once used by maharajahs famous for their opulent lifestyle.

said to be the world's largest — dole out the red tape that often ties up India in knots.

Unlike Bombay and Calcutta where film stars and rich industrialists top the social tables, New Delhi's elite consists of politicians. It is a "Who are you?" of a city. Members of parliament, aspiring politicians and senior government officials converge on private parties every night to exchange

city — automobiles, electronics and computers. Industrial development in the city doubled in the nine years to 1987 to 13.2 billion rupees.

An accommodation crisis has pushed property prices through the roof. And yet people pour in every day from surrounding areas. In 1987, municipal authorities announced that 10,000 vehicles were being

notes and gossip. Many more hang around the fringes of this culture, waiting for an invitation to join the club.

The growing wealth of the city has also given rise to a breed of nouveau riche who, unable to penetrate the enclosed world of New Delhi's politicians, descend on the city's five-star hotels, creating a completely different after-dark social scene.

New Delhi has grown at breakneck speed since the young, handsome Rajiv Gandhi became prime minister in 1984 after his mother Indira was assassinated by her Sikh bodyguards in her residence in a quiet part of the city. Since the former airline pilot took office, he has launched a policy of economic liberalization which has spawned at least three major industries in the

added to the capital's roads every month. Expensive residential areas have grown in south Delhi and around the Chanakyapuri diplomatic area where property prices match those in Europe.

But this is only half the story. Colonies of squalid huts that have sprung up like warts across the face of the city now house 1.6 million people. The residents of these *jhuggis*, which are without electricity or sanitation, are migrants who have fled poorer states in search of a living.

Like many of the civil servants and small-scale industrialists who have flocked

An artist puts the final touch to a cinema poster in Delhi (above). A group of passengers enjoy the scene on the roof of a public bus in Delhi (left). The main means of transport for India's masses the buses are always jam-packed with people.

The Taj Mahal reveals different aspects of its beguiling beauty, whether viewed from near or far. A close-up of its walls reveals intricate stone inlay (**below**). Viewed from the nearby Red Fort, it is a masterpiece of symmetry and balance (**right**).

Crisis in Agra

The health of India's famous Great White Lady, the Taj Mahal, is in danger from inside and out. She's suffering from "stone cancer" and is under constant threat from terrorists.

The white marble of the grande dame of the world's monuments, built to immortalize an emperor's love for a woman, is turning yellow with age and air pollution. Indian conservationists have warned that it may well turn black in 50 years if major steps are not taken to protect it.

Worried government officials have moved hundreds of pig iron foundries emitting thick black smoke further from the monument in Agra. But they admit that damage from the smokestacks has already taken its toll.

Two thermal power stations nearby have also been shut down. And the government has replaced coal-fired steam engines with diesel engines for trains running to and from the ancient city.

But sulfur fumes still belch daily from a government oil refinery 35 kilometers away. The refinery was set up north of Agra in Mathura in 1982 despite warnings from experts.

Perhaps most disgraceful is that for all the veneration and recognition of the monument's importance to Agra, sewage from the city's 700,000 residents still pours in daily into the Yamuna river behind the Taj. It emits a powerful stench that often blankets the romantic view

Conservationists have asked the local government to clean up the river. They also want a green belt of gardens and trees around it as a buffer against pollution.

But even then the past has caught up with the Taj. It has weathered more than 350 years of dusty winds slamming against it with tiny sand particles at speeds of up to 70 kilometers per hour.

Sharp changes in temperature — from a low of 4° C during cold winter nights to a high of 46° C during the blistering north Indian summer — have not helped either. Cracks have appeared in the giant marble slabs, caused by the iron rods expanding and contracting with the big temperature swings. Algae growth has produced black spots. The red sandstone of adjoining buildings has started to flake and discolored the monument.

Also worrying is the fact that some of the three million visitors to the monument every year are apparently overly enthusiastic to immortalize themselves along with Mumtaz Mahal. They scratch or paint their names on the rich marble. Officials say they have to keep a watchful eye for vandals.

A team of experts from UNESCO recommended in January 1988 that a limit be placed on the number of visitors to the monument to reduce carbon dioxide concentration inside. Officials say less visitors will mean less grubby hands pawing at the marble screen and structures.

Meanwhile, the Archaeological Survey of India is slowly replacing cracked or dirty slabs. They are also trying out a "clay-pack" treatment — pasting a special mixture over the marble surface to absorb chemicals and dust particles.

Perhaps the most serious threat to the Taj Mahal is the one resulting from the country's most protracted internal political problem — Sikh militancy. Sikh extremists fighting for an independent homeland have threatened to blow up the monument after the Indian Army stormed their holy shrine, the Golden Temple in Amritsar city, to flush out militants in June 1984.

Authorities have stopped night visits during moonlit evenings to the dismay of many honeymooning couples and Taj lovers. Careful bag searches are also now carried out at the entrance. Metal detectors will be introduced.

For all her fame and glory, the White Lady is struggling to maintain her youth and glory. She's fighting for her life.

here in recent years, the *jhuggi*-dwellers generally do not feel they belong to the city. They are the victims of an identity crisis caused by rapid expansion which threatens the very fabric of this changing city.

Agra is a picture of contrasts to the Indian capital despite histories that are so closely interlinked. Agra owes its place in history to the Mughals who built the massive Agra Fort and gave the world the Taj Mahal. But unlike New Delhi, Agra today is a tourist city which thrives largely on its glorious past. Many among its 700,000 population, descendants of the original builders of the Taj Mahal, make marble-inlaid replicas of the monument their forefathers had labored to erect.

Agra was a backwater until 1526 when Babur defeated the Afghan sultan, Ibrahim, Lodi, who had used the city as his capital. Babur spent most of his time expanding his empire and made no architectural contribution except for a small garden where he was buried for a few years before his remains were taken to Kabul to be permanently interred.

Until his death in 1530 Babur used Agra as the center of his military operations. But despite its importance in Mughal *realpolitik*, Babur at first was not impressed by what he saw in Agra. "We were annoyed with three things in Hindustan: one was its heat, another its strong winds, the third its dust," he wrote in his Memoirs. His son Humayun tried to found a new city in Delhi, but was thwarted by the invasion of Sher Shah Suri who also ousted the Mughals from Agra for 14 years.

It was left to Babur's illustrious grandson, Akbar the Great, to put Agra back on the map. Two years after ascending the throne at the age of 14, Akbar decided in 1558 to move the Mughal capital back to Agra. Taking a leisurely three-week cruise down the Yamuna from Delhi, he arrived on October 30, heralding the golden age of the Mughal empire.

Akbar extended his domains by military adventurism. He also made cunning political alliances through marriage which helped swell his harem to 5,000. After shaking off a power struggle within his own court in 1562, he went on to capture Kashmir in 1586, and added Sind and Orissa

in 1593. He showed remarkable tolerance toward non-Muslims. He was an enthusiastic patron of the arts and helped combine Islamic and Hindu styles.

In 1565, he gave directions for "a grand fortress such as might be worthy thereof, and correspond to the dignity of his dominions," according to his biographer Abdul Fazl. The Agra Fort of red sandstone was

completed after eight years by several thousand men and contained up to 500 palaces. Measuring 2.4 kilometers in its outer perimeter, the fort along the Yamuna was the model for subsequent Mughal forts and remains a most imposing monument in Agra today.

Even as it was being completed, Akbar began construction in 1568 of a new city, Fatehpur Sikri, after a priest there had given him blessings for a son. But the lack of water apparently forced him to return to Agra in 1584, 14 years after he had first occupied it.

*The emperor Shah Jahan was imprisoned by his son Aurangzeb in Agra's Red Fort and spent his last days gazing across the Yamuna River at the Taj Mahal (**left**). His inlaid tomb now lies alongside his adored wife at the Taj Mahal (**above**).*

The Shadow of God

One monument more than any other has come to symbolize Delhi. It is Qutb Minar, the 12th century stone tower that rises above the ruins of the ancient city.

The 72.5-meter tower stands today as the highest and best-preserved stone tower in India. It has survived earthquakes and lightning. Even more impressive is that it has withstood the idiocy of a 19th century British engineer who, in an attempt at restoration, replaced the top story with another that was so incongruous it had to be removed because it looked too much like the *topee* used by some balding British masters.

No visit to Delhi is complete without a stop at the Qutb Minar complex. The profuse Arabic script carved on the angular and circular flutings of the tower intrigue the visitor as much as the famous Iron Pillar in the courtyard below.

Like the tower, the 1,500-year-old iron column rising to a tenth of the Qutb Minar's height has mysteriously resisted the wrath of Allah. In other words, it has resisted rust. Visitors still stand with their backs to this pillar — said to have been brought to the site by Rajput rulers — and try to

Nature has spared its wrath on the Qutb Minar **(below)**. The 800-year-old soaring tower has miraculously survived earthquakes and wars and now stands above other ancient ruins on the outskirts of present-day Delhi.

wrap their hands around it. Those who succeed can hope to have their wishes fulfilled.

Work on Qutb Minar was started by Qutb-ud-Din Aibak, the ruthless founder of the first Delhi sultanate. He destroyed 27 Hindu and Jain temples in the Rajput city Qila Rai Pithora and slaughtered thousands to establish his Slave Dynasty.

Qutb was the first of a long line of Muslim rulers. He built a large mosque in the complex and designed the Qutb Minar to "cast a shadow of God over the east and over the west." Indeed, the — *monument's shadow is long at sunrise and sunset. It commemorates the sultan's victory and summons the faithful to prayer.*

Qutb-ud-Din died after finishing only the first story. Thus, historians are not sure if the tower was named after him or after another saint of that period, Qutb-ud-Din Bakhtiyar Kaki. The name could also have been derived from the Arabic word "Qutab" which means pole or axis.

Qutb-ud-Din's son-in-law and successor, Iltutmish, completed the next three storys of the tower in 1230. The tower was repaired in 1322 and again in 1368 by Tughlaq rulers after being damaged by lightning.

The open-canopied pavilion on top fell down later during an earthquake. It remained in a state of disrepair until an English engineer, Robert Smith, set about repairing the tower. Smith did marvelous work with the lower portions of the tower but failed rather miserably with the pavilion. He added an odd-looking cupola in "late Mughal style," topped by another wooden cupola which had the British flag flying above. Some of his contemporaries thought it resembled a parachute or a sahib's topee.

That cupola was itself damaged by lightning, some say because of Allah's disapproval. It was removed in 1848 and now stands in a corner of the vast mosque complex southeast of the Qutb Minar.

Notwithstanding Smith's follies, the Qutb Minar was a source of wonder and numerous pencil sketches for the British colonial masters. One, a Major Archer, even appeared to take great pride in the incongruous "topee". In the 1830s, he wrote, "There is a pavilion sort of building at the top, and a flag-staff displaying the British colors crowned the whole; this last addition was little dreamed of, when the first stone was laid."

The American writer, Robert Minturn, visited Delhi in the 1850s and called Qutb Minar "the loftiest and most remarkable column in the world."

A more remarkable architectural wonder would have been erected had Alau'd-Din Khalji, founder of the Khalji Dynasty in 1296, lived long enough. Alau'Din started work on the Alai Minar which he intended to be twice as high as the Qutb Minar. But he died just after the first story was completed. All that remains of his grand dream is the rubble under the shadow of God.

Within its walls, the Agra Fort was a city full of life though Akbar himself followed a strict regimen. Surrounded by a crack bodyguard of 20 chosen warriors, he would perform his morning devotions, then step into a balcony to show himself to his people, a Hindu custom which his successors also adopted. He acted as judge and held public audiences with many of his subjects.

and ambitious wife, Nur Jahan.

A renewed burst of architectural genius in Agra came when the greatest Mughal builder, Shah Jahan, took to the throne in 1627. He tore down many of the red sandstone buildings within the fort and erected palaces of white marble inlaid with semi-precious stones.

Shah Jahan himself lived in Khas Mahal.

In between affairs of state, he developed a passion for riding elephants, playing polo and caring for his pet leopards. He also found time to experiment with a new religion called Din Ilahi. But it failed to become popular.

Akbar died in 1605 after ruling for 49 years and was buried in a tomb he had prepared for himself at Sikandra, 120 kilometers north of Agra. His death paved the way for Jahangir who built a palace for himself but for the better part of his 22-year reign virtually abdicated his throne to his cunning

Agra thrives on its glorious past. A street vendor sells dolls clad in traditional costumes outside the city's Red Fort (above). Built in 1565 by Akbar the Great, the fortress made of red sandstone contains halls of audiences and other impressive structures.

It consisted of a large hall and two other pavilions in which his two daughters lived. He also modified the Jasmine Tower where he died after being imprisoned by his son Aurangzeb. Agra lost its influence when Shah Jahan decided to shift his capital back to Delhi in 1638 and build a new city there. But Agra's place in history was already assured. Shah Jahan had given the world the Taj Mahal.

It was a labor of love which took 20,000 men 22 years to build. The glorious marble tomb for his beloved Mumtaz Mahal (Ornament of the Palace) has become a symbol of India. The poet Tagore described it as a "teardrop in the cheek of time," while others have called it "a poem in stone" and a "monument of love."

Mumtaz, whose real name was Arjumand Shah Begum, was the second of Shah Jahan's four wives, but was clearly his favorite. She followed him on his military campaigns and stood by him through great hardship. She also bore him 14 children, dying at childbirth in 1631 in Bahanpur while accompanying him on a campaign to quell a rebellion.

ton of stone and brick masonry covered with marble. The finest craftsmen from India and Persia thronged here and an entire town called Tajganj grew up just to house the workers and their families.

Set on a square platform measuring nearly 100 square meters and surrounded by four minarets, the Taj Mahal is a masterpiece of symmetry and proportion. Every

Deeply grieved, the 39-year-old emperor shunned all amusements. His beard was said to have turned completely white. Persian historians recorded that Mumtaz asked Shah Jahan at her deathbed never to marry again and to build her a beautiful tomb. The latter was a promise he fulfilled with unparalled zeal.

Marble slabs came on bullock and camel carts from the Makrana mines in Rajasthan. They were embellished with jade from China, turquoise from Tibet, lapis lazuli from Afghanistan, coral from the Indian Ocean, cornelian from Baghdad, other precious and semi-precious stones and about 466 kilograms of gold. The core of the building of irregular hexagonal design topped by a giant dome comprises a skele-

line is measured and every brick in place. Mumtaz's tomb lies dead center under a double dome structure in the main mausoleum, surrounded by hand-carved marble screens, though her actual remains lie in an underground chamber beside the remains of her lover, Shah Jahan.

The builders never tallied up the final cost of this mammoth project. But estimates by experts have ranged between Rs 30 and 60 million. One British writer in the 1830s put it at 3.1 million pounds sterling. To maintain the monument, Shah Jahan was

*The opulent architecture of 18th century India stands in stark contrast to a villager's simple home (**above**). Here under the symbolic shadow of Akbar the Great's deserted capital, the magnificent Fatehpur Sikri, life appears unhurried – and unchanged – for centuries.*

The Baha'i House of Worship rises like an un-opened lotus flower in the Delhi landscape drawing thousands of visitors every day (**below and right**). Built by the followers of the Baha'i faith, it is a modern architectural wonder.

Bastion of the Baha'is

Not far from the madding crowd in New Delhi is another stunning marble edifice. It was built not for a woman, like the Taj Mahal, but for one of the world's newest religions, the Baha'i faith.

Set amidst sprawling lawns south of the main city, the giant marble lotus of the Baha'i House of Worship is surely one of the most artistic and spectacular modern buildings in the capital. It was built with funds donated by Baha'is in India and now towers over the surrounding landscape, beckoning followers of all faiths to join together to worship God. It is the seventh Baha'i temple in the world and arguably the most impressive.

The 10.5 hectares plot of land was bought in 1953 but building commenced only 20 years later. The marble which covers the outer shell of the lotus was donated by Greek Baha'is and cut and polished in Italy. The temple, which eventually cost nearly US$8 million, was declared open on Christmas Eve in 1986 as the Baha'i Temple for the Indian subcontinent, amid much celebration. Baha'is from across India and all over the world flocked to hear a choir chant prayers in English, Hindi and Persian.

Indians from all walks of life, rich and poor, healthy and handicapped, still troop everyday into the cavernous prayer hall of the temple. They pray in a faith which calls for tolerance, truth, faithfulness and goodwill.

The Baha'i faith was begun in Persia (now Iran) in 1844 by Baha'u'llah. Baha'u'llah was a Persian from a noble family who sacrificed wealth to proclaim the message that religious truth is not absolute but relative and that there is only one God. In 1853, he claimed to have received the first intimation of his mission as messenger of God. But he was exiled by Persian authorities to Iraq.

In Iraq in 1863, Baha'u'llah proclaimed that he was the Promised One, the Messiah, foretold by the world's religions. He was spurned again by this and other governments wherever he went. He was exiled to Constantinople and to Adrianpole. He died in Akka in 1892 at the age of 75.

The writings of Baha'u'llah include thousands of tablets (letters) that deal with a whole spectrum of issues. He had aimed to blend the world's races, nations and religions into one big family with teachings that focused on the exigencies of living in a modern world.

The faith has spread worldwide and claims 1.5 million Bahais scattered all over India. Indian Baha'is say the faith is catching on despite the pervasive influence of Hinduism.

The temple building was designed by Fariburz Shah. He chose the shape of a lotus with three sets of petals because he felt the flower is associated with several of the world's religions, notably Hinduism and Buddhism. Nine pools, interspersed with walkways, surround the temple. They represent the floating leaves of the lotus, and help to ventilate the place.

Inside, the prayer hall is an architectural masterpiece. It tapers 30.5 meters to the narrow pointed roof from its sparkling marble floor. There are no supporting columns. That gives the hall an air of breathtaking spaciousness.

The interior design is almost minimalist — wooden and marble pews set in front of a simple podium and a giant Kashmiri carpet. But more appealing is perhaps the air of calm and serenity within. Even the temperature seems to drop, cooled by the marble finish.

The nine entrances denote the different paths leading to God. Worshipers and visitors who come in through any of them take off their shoes before entering and maintain complete silence, except during prayers hours at 10 a.m. and 4 p.m. every day.

said to have set aside the revenue of 30 villages and drawn income from stalls in the bazaar at the forecourt of the Taj Mahal and from the sale of fruit in the garden.

Yet for all its beauty, it is a miracle that the Taj Mahal has survived through the centuries. Invading Jats tore off silver coins from one of the doors at the entrance when they sacked Agra in 1764. British troops stripped off the gold covering the top of the dome when they captured the city from the Marathas in 1803. During the time of Governor-General Lord Willliam Bentinck, the East India Company seriously considered tearing down the Taj Mahal and having the marble auctioned off. It was prevented only by Indian merchants who deliberately kept the price of marble low.

The site which Shah Jahan chose had be-

longed to the Hindu prince Mirza Raja Jaisingh and was exchanged for four *havelis* or mansions. Shah Jahan immersed himself totally in planning the monument, constantly conferring with his architects, engineers and had a wooden model built. The final design, in which the Iranian architect Ustad Ali included some innovations, was of unquestionable genius.

Instead of sitting dead center in a square garden called the 'char-bagh' as in traditional Mughal mausoleums, the tomb stands at the northern end of a rectangular garden measuring 540 meters by 300 me-

The enchanting beauty of the Taj Mahal makes it India's top tourist attraction, drawing thousands of visitors a day (right). But those who eke their livelihood under its shadows, such as this farmer and his bullocks (above), appear indifferent to its charms.

ters. A canal runs north-south along the splendidly-decorated garden, casting a reflection. Behind the Taj flows the Yamuna which was diverted slightly to bring it alongside the main mausoleum. It is this deviation which gives the Taj Mahal its ethereal quality.

Etched against the backdrop of a river below and blue sky with the constantly-

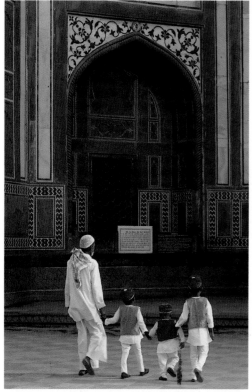

changing clouds above, the Taj Mahal evokes moods which transform themselves as it captures the changing hues of the day. At dawn, it is bathed in haunting grayish tint that slowly turns aglow with shades of pink and orange as the sun breaks its golden yolk over the horizon. The intricate details of Koranic inscriptions on the main arched entrance, the marble inlay and the handiwork on the minarets and windows come alive so slowly the transformation is indiscernible. Under Agra's punishing afternoon sun it turns into a dazzle of white. On moonlit nights the

*A man takes his grandsons for prayers (**above**), while a little boy (**right**) poses beside the flower-patterned marble-inlay work of Diwan-i-Khas in the Red Fort, Delhi. It was from here in the Diwan-i-Khas that the famous Peacock Throne was carted off in 1739.*

Taj is at its romantic best, a blur of gray, white and blue that casts a blinding spell on the beholder.

Indeed the Taj Mahal should be visited more than once. Each visit yields yet another mood, another facet. So wrote Major-General W.H. Sleeman when he visited it in 1836: "One returns and returns to it with undiminished pleasure; and though at every turn one's attention to the smaller parts becomes less and less, the pleasure which he derives from the contemplation of the greater, and of the whole collectively, seems to increase . . ." Sleeman asked his wife what she thought of it, to which she replied: "I would die tomorrow to have such another over me."

The Hindu writer Bholanauth Chundre called it "the highest architectural triumph of man" and the painter, William Hodges wrote in 1786: "The effect is such as, I confess, I never experienced from any work of art. The fine materials, the beautiful forms, and the symmetry of the whole, with the judicious choice of situation, far surpasses anything I ever beheld."

Shah Jahan must have felt the same in his final days which he spent gazing at the Taj Mahal from the Jasmine Tower in Agra Fort. He had been imprisoned there by his son Aurangzeb. He died on January 22, 1666 and his body was taken the next day on a boat to the Taj Mahal where he was buried beside his beloved.

Jean-Baptiste Tavernier, Shah Jahan's jeweller, wrote that the emperor had planned to erect a similar tomb for himself made of black marble on the other side of the river. But he was prevented from doing so by Aurangzeb. There has been, however, no conclusive evidence to suggest that this was anything more than conjecture.

Even if Shah Jahan did plan such a monument, perhaps it was best that he never erected it. The world has room for only one magical Taj Mahal, unique, captivating and beguiling, suggesting forever the singular power of love.

The builder and his beloved finally came to rest together. The tomb of Mughal ruler Shah Jahan (left) lies next to that of his beloved wife, Mumtaz Mahal, in an underground burial chamber surrounded by marble screens at the Taj Mahal.

Back of the Book

This section provides a handy, compact package of exciting insights, entertaining tidbits, and invaluable tips that will help make your trips to Delhi and Agra much more rewarding. The main maps depict Delhi and Agra and highlight some of their principal sights, districts and physical characteristics. Little-known facts about the cities from items about the unusual local language known as Indlish to the unique Eunuch community are revealed in the Trivia section. The Tours are accompanied by numbered maps that will help you get around to some of the most interesting attractions on your own. And for the adventurous, there is even a look at what can be found Off the Beaten Track. Best Bets is a digest of the best of everything that can be found in Delhi and Agra, from the top restaurants to good buys in quality dhurries. Finally, the Travel Notes provide a summary of essential travel information.

From the gates of an old mansion, the Taj Mahal is a captivating sight – an immortal beauty in respose.

Trivia

INDLISH. English is still in active use in India more than 40 years after the departure of the British, partly because India's vast population shares 14 major languages and cannot agree on a single lingua franca. Indian English, more wryly known as Indlish, has developed its unique characteristics. It combines archaic English words and phrases left over from the days of the British Raj and occasional Indian words. Indian newspapers are largely responsible for the proliferation of Indlish, which some academics warn is becoming unintelligible to all outside the subcontinent. Newspapers often carry front-page headlines such as "*Prime·Minister air-dashes across country*" or "*Thousands protest against eve-teasing.*" Few English readers outside India would understand that the Prime Minister was rushing to and fro by air, or that the protest was against sexual harrassment! Dacoits (robbers) or miscreants are often "chargesheeted" or "challaned" in court while protestors are "lathi-charged" (baton-charged) by police. The biggest culprits, however, are those writing overzealously in a language not native to them, often with disastrous results. Take this classic, for example, from one sports writer: "With bulging biceps and tremendous triceps, he was unparalleled on the parallel bars."

HIJRAS ARE THE EUNUCHS of India, who are slowly shedding their mysterious image to demand more rights after being despised for centuries. India has an estimated one million eunuchs, including 15,000 living in Delhi alone. Dressed in colorful saris, they beg for a living, going from house to house singing and dancing for a fee. Some earn a living as prostitutes. Horrific stories have been told of young boys being kidnapped and forcibly castrated by eunuch "surgeons" before being inducted into gangs. Some of these incidents have proved fatal, and the discovery of a newly-castrated youth in New Delhi in 1983 caused an uproar in the country. Eunuchs, who are said to be buried upright when they die, believe that they will be reincarnated as fertile men or women. They have formed a Hijras Organization to press for free schooling, state benefits and even representation in Parliament. None has been elected so far.

PANDEMONIUM IN PARLIAMENT often breaks out in both the upper and lower houses in India. Politicians have perfected the best and worst traditions of a legacy loosely inherited from Britain's Westminster system. Members clad in a variety of traditional Indian dresses and even sandals often yell together, march down the aisles or squat in front of the speaker to get a point across or to block a bill or motion. First-time visitors are often startled to find several parliamentarians all speaking at the same time, each trying to outshout the other. Inadvertently many chaotic sittings are adjourned until order resumes, only to start all over again the next day.

CORPSE CARRIERS. Perhaps the most unpleasant job in Delhi is that of the freelance corpse carrier. More than 30 private carriers operate in the capital, helping police remove decomposing dead bodies which even the government handlers refuse to touch. The private carriers are paid about Rs 20 to cart away each of these gruesome, maggot-ridden bodies for compulsory forensic examination and post-mortem and then to the mortuary. About 100 people die every day in Delhi.

HISTORY UNCOVERED. A long metal capsule buried underground in 1973 by the government of the late Prime Minister Indira Gandhi was unearthed four years later when she was temporarily out of power. It contained an account of India's history. The new government said the 10,000 word manuscript of India's first 25 years of independence since 1947 exaggerated the role of the Nehru family, including that of Jawaharlal Nehru, India's first Prime Minister and Indira's father. The 1.82-meter long capsule's contents were meant for posterity in the 21st century. It had been embedded in concrete inside a circular shaft dug at the walled city of Old Delhi.

BOAT CLUB is the affectionate name given to the lawns flanking Raj Path near India's Parliament, one of the greatest symbols of freedom in the world's largest democracy. That's because of the small rowboats on the shallow canal there. Demonstrations here take place at least once a week behind police barricades. They are staged by every disgruntled group imaginable — farmers, politicians, Tibetan and Afghan and Iranian refugees, students, their teachers, lawyers and doctors. All that one party needs to do is to apply for prior police permission and promise not to turn violent. Then they crowd onto the lawns where enterprising hawkers selling drinks and food ply their wares oblivious to the causes being championed. Sometimes, protestors "court arrest" by voluntarily asking police to detain them. Hundreds of

protestors are herded aboard buses and taken to police stations to have their names recorded before being released shortly after.

SACRED COWS, PART I. India's 200 million cows — worshiped by the Hindus — and 70 million buffaloes produce a staggering ONE BILLION tons of dung a year. Most is collected and dried into cakes before being used as fuel or fertilizer. A recent government scientific study said energy from cattle dung each year is equivalent to 35 million tons of coal. The government has embarked on a program to build underground biogas plants which collect fresh dung and convert it into combustible methane gas which can be connected to rural homes with pipes. Similar pilot projects are also being carried out in New Delhi to turn human night soil into energy.

SACRED COWS, PART II. Princess Irene of Greece, sister-in-law of King Juan Carlos of Spain, a cow lover, is trying to save two million European cows. She wants to bring them to India to save them from slaughter because a milk surplus is forcing Europe's farmers to kill dairy breeds. She shuttles between Spain and India raising funds and trying to convince authorities of both countries to accept her ideas.

AGRA EYESORE. Indian authorities have ordered that a giant television tower behind the Taj Mahal be removed because it is an eyesore and the source of frequent complaints by photographers visiting the marble monument.

SHAH'S REQUEST. According to a story often repeated in Agra, the last Shah of Iran was so struck by the beauty of the Taj Mahal that he requested — and was granted permission — to spend one moonlit night with his first wife inside it during a visit in the 1950s. The Archaelogical Survey of India has vehemently denied the story.

BETEL MILLIONAIRE. The ancient Indian habit of betel-chewing has spawned India's first betel millionaire. M.M. Kothari sold cigarettes at the age of 22 in 1948. But in 1973 he started making pre-packed betel concoctions, replete with lime and spices inside small plastic pouches. From a humble shophouse and an investment of Rs 12,000 (US$900), he now manufactures one

million one-rupee packets of "pan masala" a day, raking in annual sales of Rs 340 million (US$26 million.) Every street-corner shop in Delhi sells his pan masalas. However, many older Indians still prefer betel nut the traditional way — wrapped in fresh leaves by expert but grubby hands.

PREMIUM SCOTCH is highly prized in India where the government imposes high taxes on imported liquor. Scotch and soda is the standard drink for the country's upper class who often will pay high prices to secure a decent bottle. Police in Delhi have raided several illegal factories where enterprising operators fill up empty Johnnie Walker and Chivas Regal bottles with local Indian whisky and sell them as the real thing to unsuspecting drinkers — often at up to four times the original prices. The illegal bottlers pay up to Rs 50 for a good condition empty bottle with all labels undamaged and the original box still intact.

THE WRONG FOUNDATION. King George V startled everyone by announcing during the December 1911 "Delhi Durbar" gathering of maharajahs and British administrators that the capital of India was to move from Calcutta to Delhi, where a brand new city was to be built. He and Queen Mary laid the foundation stone in a northern site. But when the Planning Commission led by the architect, Sir Edwin Lutyens, arrived from London, they found it unsuitable and chose another site instead. In the stealth of one night in 1913, the commission had the foundation stone carried off on a bullock cart to Raisina Hill, where the Viceroy's House and Central Secretariat were later built.

MATCHMAKING ADVERTISEMENTS produce huge sums of income for Indian newspapers every weekend when would-be brides and grooms place several pages of ads in the classifieds. Hindus, Jains, Muslims and Christians alike in major cities advertise for prospective spouses for themselves or for their children of marriageable age. Most sought-after are Brahmin caste doctors, engineers or academics, preferably those living abroad. One zealous parent of a girl asked for a "Professionaly-qualified executive or decently-settled business match for very talented cultured beautiful girl of highly-educated affluent Agarwal family, aged 24, 160 cm tall, convent-educated, Bachelor of Commerce (Honors) with high computer education. Worldwide traveled.

Soft amiable nature. Real asset for any family. Decent marriage." Girls are often advertised as having a "wheatish complexion" to denote fair skin while men are "tall and handsome." Sometimes the advertisements are rather blunt. One "American green card holder, handsome Rajput doctor" invited correspondence from "beautiful tall girls."

AKBAR'S COPPER FOLLY. When the great Mughal emperor Akbar decided to build his capital at Agra, he ordered that the palaces of "Akbarabad" be made of copper. The 16th century Italian traveler Niccalao Manucci recorded that Akbar's builders advised him against this, saying that not enough metal could be acquired and that they would be uninhabitable because of the extreme heat in the summer and cold in the winter. "Thus, he abandoned this project, and built his palace and fortress of red hewn stones of great size," according to Manucci.

NO SEXY VEGETABLES FOR THE HAREM. The Mughal rulers kept hundreds of women in their harem. Each scarcely had the opportunity to spend more than a night every year with their emperor. They were guarded by eunuchs appointed by jealous menfolk who distrusted even their own brothers when it came to women. The Italian traveler Manucci said the bored concubine often pretended to be ill just to be able to engage in conversation and have their pulse felt by a physician through a curtain. Manucci, who claimed that he often masqueraded as a doctor to steal into the harem, wrote that the "sick" concubine would lay hold of the physician's hand, "kiss it and softly bite it. Some, out of curiosity, apply it to their breast, which has happened to me several times; but I pretended not to notice, in order to conceal what was passing from the matrons and eunuchs then present, and not arouse their suspicions." Manucci also claims that eunuchs often inspected groceries purchased for the concubines and "radishes, cucumbers or similar vegetables" were not allowed in. The 17th century English adventurer, Thomas Coryat, who traveled the world on two-pence a day, also chronicled the ban on vegetables. He said that "whatsoever is brought in of virill shape, which as instance reddishes, so great is the jealousie, and so frequent the wickedness of this people, that they are cut and jagged for feare of converting the same to some unnaturall abuse. . ."

Tours of Delhi and Agra

JAMA MASJID AND SHAHJAHANABAD. This walking tour takes you into the heart of Shahjahanabad, the walled city of Old Delhi built by the Mughals. Time appears to have stood still here. Ancient India comes alive in the sights, smells and jostle of bodies in the narrow alleys filled with an incredible array of jewelry, sweetmeats, and clothing. The main street is Chandni Chowk (Moonlit Square). It runs from the Red Fort westward to Fatehpuri Mosque. Here some of the most bloody scenes of Indian history were enacted. In 1739, the Persian invader Nadir Shah quelled a weak Mughal defence before he rode through the street and carried out an orgy of revenge killing. Up to 150,000 people died on that fateful Sunday. The scene was reenacted during the Indian Mutiny, when the victorious British exacted revenge for the loss of life during the revolt.

This tour takes you to just a few of the streets and alleys of Shahjahanabad; the rest of this endless but fascinating maze is for you to explore on your own. Start at **Digambar Jain Temple (1)** at the junction of Netaji Subhash Marg and Chandni Chowk. Outside the temple are about a dozen photographers working with fascinating, old box cameras to provide instant passport-size black and white photographs for less than Rs 2 each.

Gurdwara Sis Ganj (2) is one of the more important Sikh temples in Delhi. It was built in memory of Guru Tegh Bahadur, the ninth Sikh guru. He was beheaded by the Mughal emperor Aurangzeb in 1675. The temple is open to the public. But you must cover your head and remove your footwear to enter. The temple provides a free baggage storage service for tourists and regularly gives free meals as part of charity work. Outside, vendors sell *kirtipans*, the ceremonial swords each Sikh is supposed to carry. They make for a good souvenir.

Sonehri Masjid (3) is the old mosque next to Gurdwara Sis Ganj. Nadir Shah is said to have stood on top of the mosque directing his soldiers in the massacre of thousands in Delhi in 1739.

You can go straight to the end of Chandni Chowk to **Fatehpuri Masjid (4)**, the mosque built of red sandstone in 1650 by Fatehpuri-Begam (one of Shah Jahan's wives). But it is probably more interesting to turn off into **Dariba Kalan (5)**. This is the street of India's foremost silver merchants. Two rows of double-storied buildings are filled with dozens of them. They sell anything that could possibly be made from silver. It's a good place for interesting buys on necklaces, snuff boxes, jewelry boxes, bangles and cutlery.

Walk 150 meters further and turn right to **Kinari Bazaar (6)**, a colorful alley that should not be missed. It is here that almost every Delhi resident must come before his or her wedding day to shop for traditional finery, ranging from embroidered saris to colorful turbans and garlands made of stacks of rupee notes. Also sold here are sweetmeats wrapped in silver paper, a prized delicacy in India. Head toward **Amir Chand Marg (7)**, then turn towards **Chawri Bazaar (8)** where various crafts, including ivory work, are on sale here.

End the tour at **Jama Masjid (9)**, the largest mosque in India. Begun by Shah Jahan in 1650, it was completed in six years at a cost of Rs 1 million. The grand building, with a massive courtyard, rises from a rock and is reached by flights of steps from the east, north and south gates. The prayer hall, facing west, has 11 arches. Visitors must remove their shoes (no shorts are allowed). Tourists are not allowed in during prayers that are held at various times of the day. There are several antique shops as well as a bazaar around the mosque.

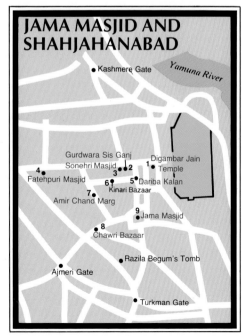

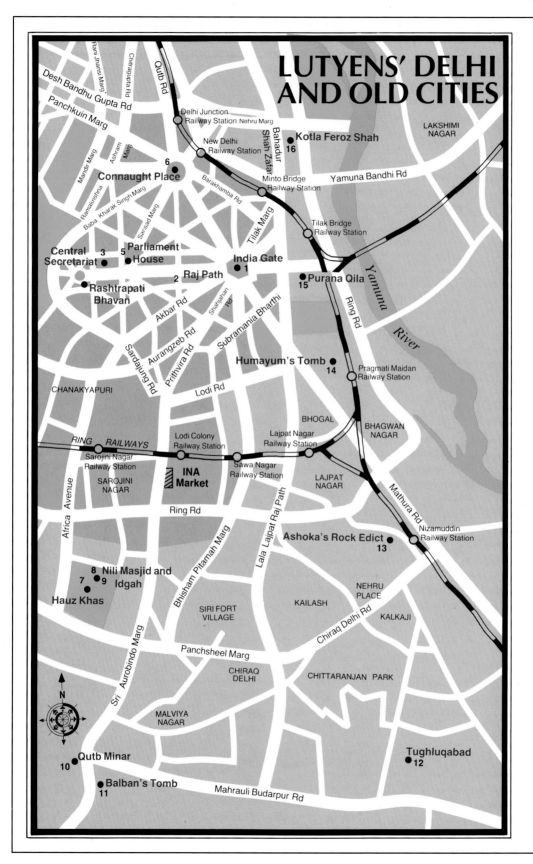

LUTYENS' DELHI AND OLD CITIES

Desh Bandhu Gupta Rd

Rani Jhansi Marg

Chitragupta Rd

Panchkuin Marg

Qutb Rd

Delhi Junction Railway Station   Nehru Marg

New Delhi Railway Station

Bahadur Shah Zafar

● **Kotla Feroz Shah**
16

LAKSHIMI NAGAR

Mandir Marg

Ashram Marg

6
● **Connaught Place**

Barakhamba Rd

Minto Bridge Railway Station

Yamuna Bandhi Rd

Ramakrishna Marg

Baba Kharak Singh Marg

Sansad Marg

Tilak Marg

Tilak Bridge Railway Station

Yamuna River

Ring Rd

Central Secretariat   3   5   **Parliament** ● **House**

● **India Gate**
1

● **Purana Qila**
15

● **Rashtrapati Bhavan**

2 **Raj Path**

Akbar Rd

Shahjahan Rd

Subramania Bharthi

Aurangzeb Rd

Prithvira Rd

Sardarjung Rd

Lodi Rd

CHANAKYAPURI

Humayum's Tomb ●
14

Pragmati Maidan Railway Station

BHOGAL

BHAGWAN NAGAR

RING   RAILWAYS

Sarojini Nagar Railway Station

Lodi Colony Railway Station

Lajpat Nagar Railway Station

Sawa Nagar Railway Station

SAROJINI NAGAR

INA Market

LAJPAT NAGAR

Africa Avenue

Ring Rd

Bhisham Pitamah Marg

Lala Lajpat Rai Path

● **Ashoka's Rock Edict**
13

Nizamuddin Railway Station

Mathura Rd

8 ● **Nili Masjid and**
7 ● ● 9   **Idgah**

Hauz Khas

NEHRU PLACE

KAILASH

KALKAJI

SIRI FORT VILLAGE

Chiraq Delhi Rd

Sri Aurobindo Marg

Panchsheel Marg

CHIRAQ DELHI

CHITTARANJAN PARK

N

MALVIYA NAGAR

● **Qutb Minar**
10

Tughluqabad
● 12

● **Balban's Tomb**
11

Mahrauli Budarpur Rd

LUTYENS' DELHI. King George V stunned his audience at the Delhi Durbar of December 12, 1911, by announcing that the capital of British India would be transferred from Calcutta to Delhi, where a brand new city was to be built. Working at a feverish pace, chief architect Edwin Lutyens and his assistant Herbert Baker, backed by tens of thousands of workers, created a city that would house the world's largest·bureaucracy and reflect the glory of the British Empire. They chose a style that blended classical Western architecture with Indian elements and went on to complete New Delhi, a city that would vie in grandeur with India's ancient cities. (The imposing red sandstone buildings, scattered on a three kilometer stretch along Raj Path, are best visited by either autorickshaw or taxi.)

Start at the eastern end of Raj Path with the **India Gate (1)**. It provides a stunning view of the Presidential Palace and the Central Secretariats. Also known as the 'All India War Memorial Arch', the 42-meter high gate was completed in 1931, well after much of the rest of the city had been built, to honor 60,000 Indians who died in World War I. The monument, similar to the Arc de Triomphe in Paris and the Marble Arch in London, is inscribed with the names of 13,516 British and Indian officers who died fighting in the Northwest Frontier and Third Afghan War.

Under the arch, an eternal flame burns alongside the inverted bayonet and helmet of the Unknown Soldier which were recent additions made after the Third Indo-Pakistan War in 1971.

Raj Path (2), or Kingsway, is the wide avenue that runs west for 3.2 kilometers. It is twice as wide as the Champs Elysees in Paris and is flanked by two canals and lined with trees. The avenue serves as the stage for a grand spectacle every year on Republic Day (January 26), when India's military hardware and culture is paraded amid much pomp and ceremony. At other times, noisy demonstrations are held regularly by an assortment of disgruntled parties, with police permission, in the lawns along the road.

The Central Secretariats (3) comprise two buildings — North and South Block. They flank the Presidential Palace and serve as government offices. Designed by Herbert Baker, the secretariats are three-stories high. Each is topped by a dome and runs for more than 400 meters. But their massive size can be appreciated only from a distance. The Prime Minister's office is in the South Block. In front of the secretariats is the Government Court and four columns presented to India by the dominions of Canada, Australia, South Africa and New Zealand.

Rashtrapati Bhavan (4), without doubt the most impressive building in Lutyens' Delhi, rises from Raisina Hill and overlooks Raj Path. Built as the Viceregal Palace, it now functions as the Presidential Palace. The domed mansion is larger than the Versailles and stands on 1.8 hectares on the midst of grounds covering 132 hectares. It has 340 rooms, 12 courtyards, a state dining room 30 meters long, eight tennis courts, cricket grounds, a nine-hole golf course and beautiful Mughal-style gardens which are a delight to visit. Although the palace is clearly Western classical in conception, the columns are carved with Indian *jaalis* and *chhattris* designs and the occasional stone elephant. Permission to visit can be obtained from the Tourist Office at 88 Jan Path. Cars and autorickshaws are allowed to drive through some of the roads in the compound.

Parliament House (5), north of Raj Path and a two-minute ride from Rashtrapati Bhavan, was not in the original plans for New Delhi. But with Indian nationalism growing in the 1920s, it was decided that a separate building housing the Legislative Assembly was necessary. The circular building, with a diameter of 171 meters is ringed with 144 pillars and houses offices, gardens, a library and a reading center and the upper and lower houses of Parliament — the bastion of the world's largest democracy.

Connaught Palace (6), north of Parliament House, was designed as the commercial center of the new city by R.T. Russell, chief architect to the government of India. Named after the Duke of Connaught, the uncle of King George V, it comprises two main concentric circles with seven radial roads that lead to a garden in the inner circle. The double-storied Georgian buildings, fronted by white columns, has become the main shopping area in Delhi and houses offices of most international airlines. Explore the area on foot, stopping off at Palika Bazaar shopping center and then turn off to Jan Path, where the main tourist shops continue.

SOME EARLY CITIES. This tour must be made by private car or taxi and takes about half a day. It takes you to some of the more prominent historical sites of early Muslim dynasties that flourished in south and east Delhi.

AGRA CITY MAP

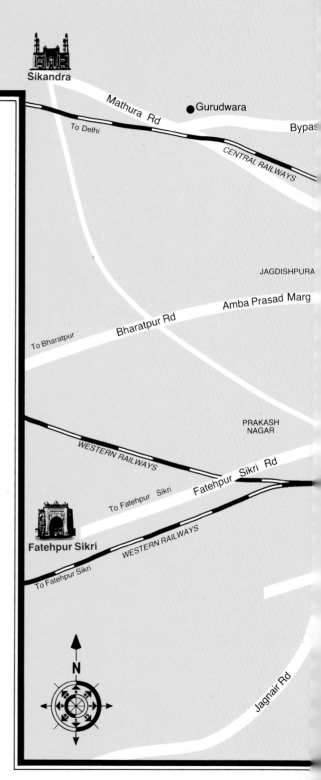

Start with **Hauz Khas (7)**, off Africa Avenue. This is a vast reservoir dug by Alau'd-Din Khaljis (1296-1316) for the inhabitants of Siri, the second city of Delhi which he founded. Now the reservoir is largely dried up and flanked partly by the double-storied colonnade of a *madrasa* or college of religious training. Nearby also lies the tomb of Feroz Shah Tughluq who died in 1388. There is a huge park north of Hauz Khas and here in this serene green lung can be found deer and peacock as well as the ruins of several tombs. The major Muslim tombs or mosques scattered northeast of the reservoir are **Nili Masjid (8)**, built in 1506 during the reign of Sikander Lodi; and **Idgah (9)**, the remnants of a battlement and mosque built during the Tughluq dynasty.

Drive south towards Sri Aurobindo Marg and head for **Qutb Minar (10)**, the imposing Tower of Victory which is considered the symbol of Delhi. At this complex, Qutb-ud-Din Aibak, who founded what became known as the Slave Dynasty, leveled 27 temples to build Quwwat-ul Islam mosque in 1193, India's earliest extant mosque. Other notable monuments here are the tomb of Iltutmish; Alau'd-Din's tomb and college; the south gateway known as Alai Darwaza; the Alai Minar, the giant rubble base of what was intended as a tower much taller than the Qutb Minar; and an iron pillar of Hindu origin dating back to the fourth century.

Turn off at **Balban's tomb (11)** on the western side of the Mehrauli bypass. Here, in an immaculately-tended park, lies the domeless square chamber believed to be the tomb of Ghiyathu'd-Din Balban (1265-1287), a ruler of the Slave Dynasty. There is also the Jamali-Kamali mosque, south of Balban's tomb. It was built round 1528 for Jamali, a saint and poet who lived during the end of the Lodi dynasty.

Double-back to the Mahrauli-Badarpur road and head east towards **Tughluqabad (12)**, the magnificent fortress that was the site of the third city of Delhi. Set on an octagonal plan with a 6.5 kilometer perimeter, the fortress, built by Ghiyath'd-Din Tughluq between 1321 and 1325 is surrounded by imposing ramparts which slope downwards. The palaces and reservoirs have largely crumbled, but Tughluqabad remains as perhaps the most spectacular of Delhi's old cities. There are still underground chambers which could have served either as granaries or dungeons. The high mounds and bastions provide a splendid view of Delhi on a clear

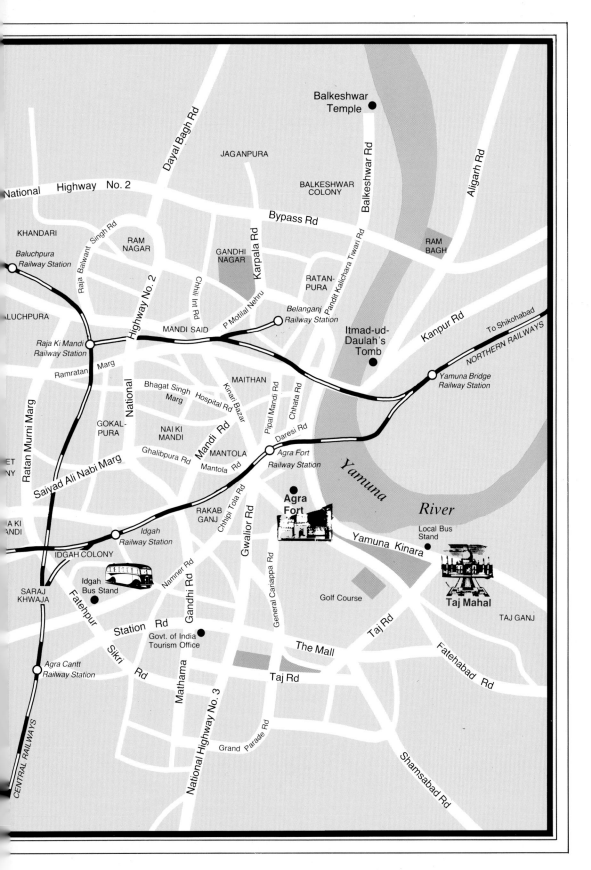

day. Walk along a two-meter wide causeway, once used by the king's horsemen, to the main mausoleum containing the remains of Ghias-ud-Din, his wife and his son. Then head north towards **Ashoka's Rock Edict (13)**. Discovered in 1966, the engravings on a rockface are an important record of the Maurya emperor Ashoka (273-236 BC). The ten lines in Brahmi script and Prakrit language comprise an epigraph about how Ashoka helped bring people closer to the gods.

Humayun's tomb (14) was built by his widow Bega Begam nine years after his death in 1565. It is the first substantial example of Mughal architecture. Several members of the Mughal royal family are buried in this tomb. The last Mughal emperor Bahadur Shah II took shelter here during the Indian Mutiny in 1857 before he was captured by a Major Hodson and exiled to Burma by the British.

Purana Qila (15), raised in the 16th century, is said to be built over the site of an ancient city in Delhi. It occupies a mound said to conceal the ruins of Indraprastha, the capital of the Pandavas, described in the great Indian epic *Mahabharata*. Fine earthenware, known among archaeologists as the Painted Grey Ware, dating back to 1,000 BC was discovered here. The ramparts and fortress which stand above the original city were built by the Persian invader Sher Shah Suri, who snatched power from the Mughals briefly (1538-1545), destroying some earlier Mughal architecture, before Humayun defeated him and regained control. Excavations between 1969 and 1973 have also unearthed artifacts from the Mauryan (circa 300 BC) up to the late Mughal periods.

Some of the buildings still standing within the complex are the Qala-i-Kuhna Masjid (Mosque of the Old Fort) built by Sher Shah in 1541; and Sher Mandal, a two-storied octagonal tower which is believed to have been used as a library. It is here that Humayun is said to have fallen from the steps to his death.

Drive further north to **Kotla Feroz Shah (16)**, the fifth city of Delhi, built by Feroz Shah Tughluq (1351-88), who also built Hauz Khas. Standing on the banks of the Yamuna River, the citadel comprises three rectangular enclosures built of rubble and aligned on the eastern wall. One of the buildings still standing inside the complex is the Jami Masjid, one of the largest mosques in the Tughluq era. Nearby, standing atop a pyramidal structure is the Ashokan column, a stone column inscribed

with Ashoka's edicts. It was brought by Feroz Shah from Topra in the Ambala district.

AGRA FORT. The imposing Agra was the model for subsequent Mughal forts. Akbar started building it in 1565 on the site of another older fort. His son and grandson modified it. Each left behind his own distinct styles and tastes but Akbar's influence stands out strongest. It was intended as an impenetrable fortification, but succumbed to several invasions. The latest was by the British in the 19th century. Lying west of the Yamuna like a giant belly, the fort has a perimeter of 2.4 kilometers and contains numerous buildings which are a delight to explore. Open sunrise to sunset, the entrance fee is Rs 2 except on Fridays when it is free (but beware of the huge crowds on that day).

Begin with the **Amar Singh Gate (1)**, the southern entrance to the fort. It was built by Shah Jahan in honor of the Rajput hero Amar Singh Rathore, the maharajah of Jodhpur. An interesting story surrounds the gate: In 1644, in the full court of Shah Jahan, Amar Singh killed the imperial treasurer Salabat Khan who had insulted him. Amar Singh fled on horseback as soldiers pursued him. Then he jumped off the high wall at the gate, killing himself and the horse. (Another version relates that he and the horse survived the jump and fled for some 10 kilometers before being caught up.)

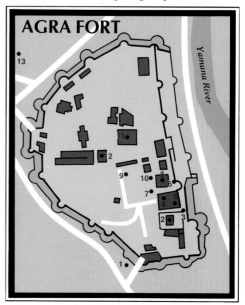

AGRA FORT

Jahangir's Palace (2) is an exquisite, double-storied structure of red sandstone filled with intricate carvings that clearly show strong Hindu influence. An open-hall with 14 richly-carved pillars and brackets supports a remarkably beautiful roof. It was at one time covered with paintings of gold and other brilliant colors.

Khas Mahal (3) was built entirely of marble by Shah Jahan over an earlier building. It comprises three pavilions. The central one is his drawing and sleeping room. In it, there is a tank where fountains once spewed jets of water day and night. The hall was originally adorned with paintings of Mughal emperors, which, like the gold plating on the ceiling, were scraped off.

The central pavilion is flanked by two others shaped like palanquins which served as the residence of Shah Jahan's two daughters, Roshan Ara and Jahan Ara. It is said that Shah Jahan did not allow them to marry for fear of more rivalry to his throne, but built them palanquin palaces topped with golden colored roofs to make up for the misery of confinement and provide the illusion that they were always traveling around.

In front of Khas Mahal lies **Angoori Bagh (4)** or Grape Garden, laid out by Akbar for his empress and other ladies of the court with soil said to have come from Kashmir. The tank here is said to have been used by the harem for bathing.

Sheesh Mahal (5), the Palace of Mirrors, was built in 1632 by Shah Jahan as a Turkish bath for his harem. It had a tank for hot water and another for cold water. Covered with countless mirrors inside, the emperor is said to have delighted himself peeping at the innumerable reflected images of the ladies bathing and changing.

Samman Burj (6), the Jasmine Tower, was built by Jahangir according to the wishes of his empress Nur Jahan. Finished with excellent carvings, marble inlay and finely-carved screens, the octagonal tower was modified by Shah Jahan and served as the residence of his favorite wife, Mumtaz Mahal. It was here that Shah Jahan was kept a prisoner by his son, Aurangzeb, who deposed him in 1659. Shah Jahan died here in January 22, 1666, gazing at the Taj Mahal and pining for his beloved. Aurangzeb later built **Meena Masjid (7)**, a white marble mosque, for his imprisoned father.

Diwan-i-Khas (8), the Hall of Private Audience, is made of pure white marble by Shah Jahan in 1637. It was here that the emperor conducted morning and evening meetings with his cabinet and met visiting dignitaries. **Diwan-i-Am (9)**, a colonnaded red-sandstone building, served as the Hall of Public Audience where durbars were held every morning to hear cases and grant favors. A cannonball fired by General Perron in 1803 tore a hole through the screen which can still be seen.

Machchi Bhavan (10), a red sandstone situated between the Diwan-i-Khas and Diwan-i-Am. It was once covered with marble tanks filled with colorful fish in the days of Shah Jahan. The buildings surrounding the courtyard are said to have housed the royal treasury. But the marble tanks were dug out by invading Jats in the 1760s while fragments of the buildings were torn out and sent to England during the time of Lord Hastings.

Moti Masjid (11), the Pearl Mosque, was built of white marble north of the Diwan-i-Am by Shah Jahan at a cost of Rs 300,000 between 1647 and 1654. Three gates lead to the mosque which can hold 570 worshipers and has chambers for the women separated by screens. The name is said to be taken from a huge pearl that once hung on a golden chain from the ceiling.

Ladies' Bazaar (12), served as an open-air market built by Akbar for use of the ladies of the court. The wives and daughters of the Hindu nobility used to meet regularly to buy and sell cloth and jewelry here. No one was allowed except Akbar who often disguised himself as an old woman to mingle among the ladies and pick out the pretty ones to add to his harem, a practice which irked the Rajput chiefs and nobles so much that many of them stopped allowing their womenfolk to partake in the bazaar.

Jami Masjid (13), which stands in front of Agra fort railway station, was built by Shah Jahan between 1644 and 1649 according to the wishes of one of his daughters.

FATEHPUR SIKRI. The great Mughal emperor Akbar (1542-1605) left his distinct imprint in Fatehpur Sikri. It was built as his capital city but abandoned after several years, apparently because of a water shortage. The ghost town 38 kilometers from Agra was built in 1569 by Akbar who had sought blessings for a son from a Muslim priest in the then obscure village. Hire a taxi or take one of several buses that leave Agra daily to get to Fatehpur. This tour takes you around some of the

more interesting buildings within this fascinating city, the most perfectly-preserved Mughal palatial city which crystallized a unique period in Mughal history.

The writer E.V. Lucas (1868-1935) said of Fatehpur: "All Shah Jahan's creations — the Taj, the marble mosque, the palaces both here and at Delhi, even the great Jama Masjid at Delhi, have a certain sensuous quality. They are not exactly decadent, but they suggest sweetness rather than strength. The Empire had been won and Shah Jahan could indulge in luxury and ease. But Akbar had to fight, and he remained to the end a man of action, and we see his character reflected in his stronghold Fatehpur Sikri, which one visits from Agra and never forgets."

Enter through **Agra Gate (1)** on the east and go past **Tansen Mahal (2)**, the red sandstone pavilion that was once the home of Akbar's court musician, Tansen, but which now serves as the quarters and office of the Archaeological Survey of India. **Naubatkhana (3)**, The Place Where Drums Are Beaten, is a square building with four gates from which an imperial band used to herald Akbar's arrival to the Hall of Public Audience. The musicians also played at certain hours of the day to announce time. Gold and silver coins were minted at the **Mint (4)** and stored in the treasury (now a ruined building on the other side of the road).

Diwan-i-Am (5), the Hall of Public Audience, is a spacious rectangular hall where the emperor met his subjects. The royal harem used to watch the

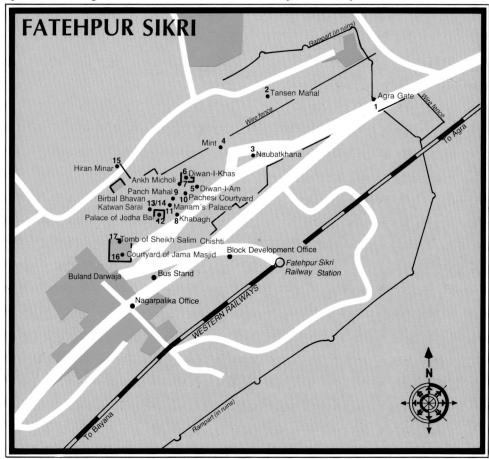

FATEHPUR SIKRI

- Rampart (in ruins)
- 2 Tansen Mahal
- Wire fence
- 1 Agra Gate
- Wire fence
- To Agra
- Mint 4
- 3 Naubatkhana
- 15 Hiran Minar
- 6 Diwan-I-Khas
- Ankh Micholi
- 7
- 5 Diwan-I-Am
- Panch Mahal 9
- 10 Pachesi Courtyard
- Birbal Bhavan
- 13/14 Mariam's Palace
- Katwan Sarai
- 11
- Palace of Jodha Bai 12
- 8 Khabagh
- 17 Tomb of Sheikh Salim Chishti
- 16 Courtyard of Jama Masjid
- Block Development Office
- Buland Darwaja
- Bus Stand
- Fatehpur Sikri Railway Station
- Nagarpalika Office
- WESTERN RAILWAYS
- To Bayana
- Rampart (in ruins)
- N

proceedings from latticed screens on the sides of the hall as Akbar presided over the hearings. Those convicted of death were said to have been trampled to death by an elephant tied to a giant ring which can still be seen in the garden in front of the hall. **Diwan-i-Khas (6)**, the Hall of Private Audience, is a curious building with strong Hindu characteristics. Viewed from the outside it appears to be a double-storied building but inside it comprises one large chamber with an octagonal column in the center, on top of which is a platform enclosed by latticed screens. From here the emperor showed himself everyday to his subjects. Some refused to eat until they saw his face. The central column shows a blend of Muslim, Hindu, Jain and Christian motifs.

Ankh Micholi (7) was where Akbar was said to have played hide and seek with the harem though historians believe it probably served as a storage for records. **Kwabagh (8)**, Akbar's sleeping chambers, was originally decorated with golden ornamentation but fell into ruin until it was partially restored by Lord Curzon in 1905. **Panch Mahal (9)**, or Wind Tower, is a five-story building that tapers in size at the top and is built in a Buddhist style. Akbar and his ladies used to climb up the stairs of the Panch Mahal to enjoy the cool breeze. From the roof, one gets a spectacular view of most of Fatehpur Sikri. The **Pachesi Courtyard (10)**, in front of the Panch Mahal, was built as a giant chessboard. The ladies of the court were said to have been used as living pieces. " The pieces were all female slaves splendidly dressed, and whosoever won carried off the sixteen ladies," said the English writer Emily Eden.

Mariam's Palace (11), the quarters of one of Akbar's wives, Mariam-Uz-Zamani, has profuse carvings and distinct Hindu motifs. **Jodha Bai ka Mahal (12)** is a double-storied palace of Jodha Bai, the Hindu wife of Akbar's son. **Birbal Bhavan (13)** was built by Raja Birbal, Akbar's prime minister, for his daughter. It has an ornately-carved roof and blends Hindu and Muslim architecture. Adjoining Birbal Bhavan is the **Katwan Sarai (14)**, a large courtyard which was used by visiting merchants. From Birbal Bhavan, you can get a clear view of the **Hiran Minar (15)**, or "Deer Tower" built above the remains of Akbar's favorite elephant. It is a 26-meter tower from which numerous elephant tusks protrude.

Jama Masjid (16), built as a copy of the Grand Mosque in Mecca, was completed in 1572 at a cost of Rs. 500,000 then. In the giant courtyard of the mosque is the **Tomb of Sheikh Salim Chishti (17)**, the priest who blessed Akbar with sons before dying in 1571. Akbar originally built the tomb with red sandstone, but it was covered with marble during the time of Jahangir. Inside the cenotaph is inlaid with intricate mother-of-pearl and surrounded by perforated marble screens.

Off the Beaten Track

THE RAIL TRANSPORT MUSEUM has a collection of antique Indian trains. Most are steam engines and old wooden coaches built during the days of the British Raj and used by maharajahs or viceroys. Look for the coach built for the Prince of Wales (later Edward VII) when he visited India in 1876. The museum is a treasure house for train freaks that also offers a toy train ride around the open-air exhibits. There is also a collection of train memorabilia covering the gamut of the colorful history of trains in India. Open 9:30 a.m. to 5:30 p.m. except Mondays. Admission is Rs 2.

INDIRA GANDHI MEMORIAL. One woman more than any other has transformed post-independence India: Indira Gandhi, the shrewd daughter of India's first Prime Minister, Jawaharlal Nehru. She governed India for almost two decades until she was killed by her own bodyguards on October 31, 1984 at her home at 1 Safdarjang Rd. The home has now been converted into a memorial. Hundreds of Indians come daily on a sort of pilgrimage to the New Delhi memorial to see how she lived and where she was assassinated, but unfortunately it has been left out of most tour itineraries. It's a must for those interested in modern Indian history.

SURAJ KUND. Twenty kilometers from New Delhi is the mysterious amphitheater and sun pool of Suraj Kund, said to be the only ancient Hindu monument around Delhi not destroyed by invading Muslims. The temple is believed to have been built in the 10th century by Raja Suraj Pal, one of the chieftains of the Toma clan, who were sunworshipers. The complex, and an adjoining reservoir where boating and fishing are permitted, is reached after a pleasant drive across the border between New Delhi and Haryana state. A hotel and a motel are located next door.

JANTAR MANTAR. Tucked away in the middle of New Delhi, along Parliament Street, is an intriguing astronomical observatory built in 1724 by Raja Jai Singh II, a Hindu ruler who was obsessed with the stars. An astute king and one of the brightest minds of India, Jai Singh explored the universe by borrowing and improving on western and eastern scientific knowledge. He modelled his observatory after the Persian astronomer Mirza Ulugh Beg's 15th century observatory at Samarkand, constructing giant stone and cement structures. A sundial with a 20.7-meter axis wall which casts a shadow to chart time is said to be accurate to within two seconds. Much of the original marble which covered the structures was damaged by invading Jats, but the observatory is otherwise generally well-preserved. Jai Singh built similar observatories in Jaipur, Varanasi, Ujjain and Mathura.

BAHAI TEMPLE. The lotus-shaped marble temple of the Bahais, located in the southern suburbs of New Delhi, is one of the most spectacular pieces of modern architecture in modern India.

THE NATIONAL MUSEUM has a stunning collection of ancient Indian artifacts, ranging from Stone Age implements to 19th century brass statuettes. The museum is on Jan Path in New Delhi. One interesting section is the Greek and Roman sculpture of the 4th century A.D. unearthed from the Gandhora region in present day Afghanistan and Pakistan where Alexander the Great's army invaded before returning home — but not before leaving behind some artisans and sculptors who left their mark. The museum is open between 10 a.m. and 5 p.m. and there are conducted tours everyday at 10:30 a.m., 11.30 a.m., noon, 2 p.m., 3:30 p.m. and daily film shows at 11:30 a.m., 2:30 p.m., and 4 p.m..

THE INTERNATIONAL DOLLS MUSEUM is a vast and interesting collection of several thousand dolls, mostly Indian, from nearly 100 countries. The museum is on Bahadur Shah Zafar Marg. Open 10 a.m. to 6 p.m. daily except Mondays.

TIBET HOUSE. The Tibetan spiritual leader, the Dalai Lama, fled to India in 1959 after an abortive uprising against Chinese rule in Lhasa. The small Tibet House museum at 16 Jor Bargh contains some of the ceremonial items with which the mysterious "god-king" fled into exile with. Tibetan handicrafts are also sold here and there are regular discussions by Tibetan exiles, most of whom are very intense about religion and politics.

NIZAMUDDIN VILLAGE is a medieval Muslim village in the heart of New Delhi. Entering it is like walking through a time warp into the past of at least 600 years ago. Bearded men smoking hookahs still sew goatskin waterbags by hand, or sell buffalo meat along the narrow alleys winding around the tomb of Hazrat Nizamuddin, a famous poet who died in 1325 at the age of 92. The present structure, built in 1562 upon the site of the original tomb which no longer exists, comprises an intricately-painted square chamber surrounded by verandahs with arches. Next to the tomb is the Jama'at-Khana-Masjid, a mosque which was built in 1325 and is now the oldest building in the area.

LODI GARDENS. Four kilometers south of Connaught Circus lie the sprawling and manicured lawns of Lodi Gardens, one of the best kept parks in Delhi. Originally named Lady Wilingdon Park, it is quiet and peaceful, filled with flower shrubs and shady trees. Inside is the tomb of a Sayyid ruler and three tombs of Lodi kings. The two Afghan dynasties flourished between 1414 and 1526, until Babur defeated the Lodis and founded the Mughal dynasty. The gardens are in the center of a posh residential district next to the United Nations office, and are popular with joggers.

OLD DELHI. Shahjahanabad, the 7th city of Delhi, was once enclosed by walls. Most have been destroyed through the ages, but the gates remain. Chandni Chowk, the main street, stretches from the Red Fort westwards for more than one kilometer to Fatehpuri Mosque. Little has changed since the days of Shah Jahan in the 17th century, and the warren of alleys filled with shops and crowded bazaars still beckon the visitor. Every alley is a discovery in itself where everything from antiques and food to Indian jewelry is sold.

SUNDAY BAZAAR. Probably the biggest in Delhi, is held every Sunday behind the Red Fort. Stretching for 800 meters along Mahatma Gandhi Road, it offers every conceivable item, from brassieres to brassware to broken clocks. It is where every piece of junk thrown out by a Delhi housewife seems to finally end up. Nothing much to be bought from here, but strolling through the countless number of stalls gives an interesting insight into bazaars in Delhi.

METCALFE HOUSE is not far from Delhi University, at the northern end of Mahatma Gandhi Road. It was built in 1835 in early Indo-European style for Sir Thomas Metcalfe, British Resident of the Mughal Court, an eccentric man who transferred all his family treasures to India. Metcalfe died in 1853 in this house, which was later occupied by his son, Sir Theophilus, a key figure in the 1857 mutiny. The building, which has a unique blend of architecture, changed hands several times and is now the property of the Indian government.

SULTAN GHARI'S TOMB is one of the first examples of Muslim mausoleums in India. It is located eight kilometers west of Qutb Minar. Iltut-

mish built it in 1231 for his son and heir apparent, Nasiru'd-Din Mahmud, who died in 1229 while fighting a war for Iltutmish. The colonnaded structure was built partly from the remains of Hindu temples which were destroyed.

SAFDARJANG'S TOMB AND MOTH KI MASJID. One of the finest and last examples of Mughal architecture is the tomb of Safdarjang built in 1754 by his son. Nearby is Moth ki Masjid, which is built on a raised platform surrounded by walls. It was constructed by Miyan Bhuwa who served as minister to two Lodi kings, Sikander (1488-1517) and Ibrahim (1517-26). He was killed for incurring the wrath of Ibrahim. Legend says that Sikander once picked up a grain of *moth* (a kind of lentil) from another mosque and handed it over to the minister who sowed it. The grain multiplied manifold until there was sufficient money from the proceeds to build the mosque which was given its present name.

SIKANDRA. Ten kilometers north of Agra lies the tomb of Akbar, set in the midst of a large square garden at Sikandra. Akbar started building it but died before its completion, leaving his son to do the rest of the work. The five-story mausoleum is made entirely of sandstone except for the top tower, with the real tomb in the lowest mortuary chamber. There is also a cenotaph on the fifth story and a recently discovered secret tomb hidden in the fourth floor; its purpose is still uncertain.

ITMAD-UD-DAULAH, situated across the Yamuna River in Agra, is the delicate mausoleum said to have inspired Shah Jahan to build the Taj Mahal. It was the first mausoleum said to be completely covered in marble and inlay work. The squat building covered with striking patterns of mustard and black colors, was built between 1622 and 1628 by Nur Jahan, Jahangir's wife, for her father Mirz Ghiyas Beg, an able man who had traveled from Iran to seek his fortune in the Mughal court and went on to become the Imperial Treasurer.

CHINA-KA-RAUZA. One kilometer north of Itmad-ud-Daulah lies China-ka-Rauza, which was constructed in the early 17th century by Azfal Khan, a senior official of Shah Jahan. The design of the short tomb with its large dome structure has a heavy Persian influence, though much of it has fallen to ruin. The rectangular structure is the only example of Mughal architecture using glazed tiles (from which the name of the tomb is derived.)

RAM BAGH, or the "Garden of Leisure and Rest", two kilometers north of China-ka-Rauza, is the earliest Mughal garden in India. It was laid out by Babur, the founder of the Mughal empire, on the left bank of the Yamuna River in 1528 and set the stage for further architecture endeavors by his descendants. The garden was used as a favorite place of recreation by Babur, who was buried here briefly before his remains were brought back to Kabul to be permanently interred. It was also used by his great grandson Jahangir and his wife. (Itmad-ud-Daulah, China-ka-Rauza and Ram Bagh can be reached by cycle rickshaw from central Agra).

KEOLADEO NATIONAL PARK. Fifty-four kilometers from Agra lies the bird sanctuary of Bharatpur. Established in 1956 on 30 square kilometers of swamp, more than 300 species of birds fly here for spot breeding in September and October and winter migration from November and February. A good time to go is January and February (preferably at dawn and dusk and armed with binoculars and sweaters) when the rare Siberian crane makes its visit. The park used to be a shooting gallery for the maharajahs and viceroys, with Viceroy Lord Linlithgow taking top honors for downing 4,273 ducks in 1938. Visitors can stay at Bharatpur Forest Lodge which has 18 rooms.

RANTHAMBORE TIGER RESERVE. Halfway between Bharatpur and Kota is the Ranthambore Tiger reserve in Rajasthan state. Spread over 400 square kilometers of dry forest, it is home to hundreds of tigers which have multiplied thanks to Project Tiger, a conservation scheme launched by the World Wildlife Fund in 1973 to save the big cats. The reserve is accessible by train from Delhi and by car from Delhi and Agra. The best time to go is between March and May, just before the onset of the monsoons. Hire a jeep and go tiger-spotting either at dawn or dusk.

SARISKA WILDLIFE SANCTUARY. Situated 200 kilometers from Delhi, the Sariska game park is situated in a valley filled with deer, wild boar, tigers, leopards and bears. At the Kaligati ranger post, visitors can climb a tower to spot and photograph animals gathering at a waterhole nearby. There are several places to stay, including Tiger Den Tourist Bungalow, Forest Rest House and Hotel Sariska Palace, which was once a maharajah's hunting lodge.

Best Bets

DELHI

COFFEE AND TEA SETS made of 90 per cent silver or "white metal" — an alloy of copper, zinc and nickel with silver-plating — are worth buying. Check out the shops along Jan Path, Connaught Place and Sundar Nagar. An incredible range of silver jewelry can also be found at Dariba Kalan off Chandni Chowk in Old Delhi.

A WIDE RANGE OF INDIAN CRAFTS, brass and copper ware, furniture and linen from various states can be found at Central Cottage Industries Emporium. Items can be packed and shipped with little hassle. The state emporia along Baba Kharak Singh Marg off Connaught Circus also offer a wide range of crafts and fabrics from various states. Especially commendable is the Gujarat Emporium. The Sundar Nagar shopping area near the Oberoi Intercontinental also has an excellent range of artifacts, especially from Rajasthan state. Though pricier, the quality is generally higher than elsewhere. Look out for Rajasthan furniture (low tables and chairs made of wood and copper) and circular, wooden flour grinders from Gujarat which can be turned into side-tables.

BRASS AND COPPER items, other than the standard fare in Jan Path, can be found at Swami Copper and Brass Palace at 13 Yashwant Place. It offers interesting old and new artifacts. Prices here are also negotiable and artifacts can be polished and delivered within a day or two at no extra cost.

GOOD QUALITY IVORY is sold at the Ivory Mart in Chawri Bazaar behind Jama Masjid in Old Delhi. There you can also watch skilled craftsmen at work.

FABRICS OF ALL KINDS can be found in India. Most are handmade. Silk from Bihar, Kashmiri crewel work, *khadi* (handwoven and printed wool) and cotton and silk embroidery (often with decorative small mirrors from Rajasthan and Gujarat are all excellent items for clothes, home decora or gifts. Central Cottage Industries Emporium still comes out tops for the sheer range, but interesting buys can be made at the smaller shops along Jan Path and the state emporia. For linen, tablecloths and curtains, go to Fabindia, N-Block, Great Kailash. Excellent saris, embroidery and colorful headgear for fancy-dress parties may be obtained at Kinari Bazaar (near Chandni Chowk, turn off from Dariba Kalan), which specializes in Indian wedding garments.

DHURRIES are hand-woven woolen or cotton rugs made mostly in north India. Cottage Industries offers a variety of dhurries and carpets ranging from Indian to Western designs. The purchase of carpets needs some expert help so it is advisable to go with someone who knows about them. Most carpets are made of silk (natural silk being more expensive than synthetic silk), cotton, wool and a combination of these materials. The price depends on the size, design, number of knots and materials used. One shop worth trying out is Yak International, 44 Ring Road, Lajpat Nagar-111. They have a showroom at Kanishka Hotel along Ashoka Road but prices are lower at the Ring Road warehouse. Shyam Ahuja at 3 Local Shopping Centre, Block-E, Masjid Moth, Greater Kailash II (near Savitri Cinema) has top-rate dhurries, quilts, bedspreads and cushion covers. Prices are high but quality here is assured.

INDIA IS THE WORLD'S LARGEST TEA PRODUCER and home to the Darjeeling brands which are sold widely in New Delhi. For a good selection, try Tea City, 133 Sarojini Nagar Market, a "tea supermarket" where products are packed in neat, airtight dispensers.

FOR THOSE WHO PREFER COFFEE, India produces quality brands from the southern states packed and sold by the government, although few people realize it. For beans or crushed powders that you can take home, go to the Coffee Board at 66 Tolstoy Lane (opposite Central Cottage Industries on Jan Path).

LEATHER GOODS are definitely a good buy in India. Because sheep leather and skilled labor are abundant, prices are low. Yashwant place at Chanakyapuri has become the top leather market in New Delhi and good buys can be found here for western-style leather jackets, bags and even fur coats. Quality in this shopping center varies but Hidesign Creations at 6-A Yashwant Place offers good workmanship at reasonable prices. Mintini's at E-12 Connaught Place has the reputation as one of the best leather shops in New Delhi but prices here are higher than in Yashwant Place. For belts, shoes, and handbags made from various kinds·of leather, try Regal Shoe Shop at Ashoka Hotel.

PERFUMES, TOO, are a major industry in India. Try Heaven of Perfumes at 15 Yashwant Place. Prices here are a fraction of those of top brand names. The bottles may not be as fancy, but the scents are comparable.

FRAMING for pictures and prints is the specialty at Bharat Plywood Company, K-22 Connaught Circus, opposite the Plaza Cinema.

SAMPLE NORTH INDIAN AND MUGHLAI FOOD at all deluxe hotels. They offer moderate to excellent versions at relatively high prices. Especially commendable are Bukhara at the Maurya Sheraton, Handi at the Taj Palace and Haveli at the Taj Mahal. Outside the hotels, there are several clean restaurants that serve quality food at lower prices. Moti Mahal Restaurant, at Netaji Subhas Marg, Darya Ganj, near Delhi Gate, is a large open-air restaurant that specializes in tandoori and butter chicken. Only Rs. 40 for an entire bird. It's open 9 a.m. to midnight except Tuesdays. Khyber Restaurant at Kashmere Gate also offers superb butter chicken and mutton *barra* at similarly reasonable prices. The two-storied air-conditioned restaurant is open seven days a week from 10 a.m. to 11 p.m.

SOUTH INDIAN FOOD is probably best at Dasaprakash at the Ambassador Hotel at Sujan Singh Park. Woodlands at the Lodi Hotel along Lala Rajpat Lai Marg is also worth trying.

CHINESE FOOD is abundant. But most Chinese restaurants in major Indian cities offer an Indianized version of Chinese cuisine: overcooked and drowned in sauces. But an increasing number of Chinese chefs from Hong Kong and Singapore have come to India to work in the restaurants of the top hotels. What they serve, mostly Cantonese and some Szechuan, compares with the finest Chinese food anywhere in the world. They include: Pearls at the Hyatt Regency; Taipan at the Oberoi Intercontinental; the Golden Phoenix at Le Meridien, Tea House at Taj Palace; and, The House of Ming at the Taj Mahal. If you relish Huo Kuo (Mongolian hot-pot), then go to Chungwa, D-13 Defence Colony.

CONTINENTAL FOOD is also found in many places in many versions of varying quality. Classy and pricey Italian fare is served at Valentinos at the Hyatt, French at Le Pierre at Le Meridien and a mixture of French, Spanish and Italian at Orient Express at the Taj Palace where the decor simulates the vintage Paris-Istanbul train. Pickwick's at Claridges Hotel maintains its old world charm and gives solid value for money for a full western meal.

YES, THE FAST FOOD CRAZE has also infiltrated India, albeit with a local flavor. The Nirula

chain offers the usual western selection of hamburgers (but made from mutton), pizzas and ice-creams in air-conditioned restaurants which have become havens for New Delhi's middle-class.

DISCOS, TOO, have arrived. They are usually at their liveliest on Friday and Saturday nights after 10. The top of the line is Oasis at the Hyatt, where the decor is classy and the music superb. It's open from 6 p.m. to 2 a.m. Ghungroo at the Sheraton is open from 10 p.m. to 3 a.m. and is popular with teenagers.

BOOKSTORES can be found in Connaught Place which has several good ones around Inner Circle, notably New Book Depot at B-18; Picadilly Book Store at 64 Shanker Market, Connaught Circus; and Oxford Book and Stationery Company, Scindia House, Connaught Circus. Books, both foreign and local, are marketed inexpensively in India and definitely worth picking up for your library or coffee table.

MAPS OF DELHI AND AGRA can be obtained from the map section of the Archaeological Survey of India, next to Central Cottage Industries Emporium on Jan Path. For maps of India in general, ask for Bartholomew's map of India, Pakistan, Nepal, Bangladesh and Sri Lanka at bookshops.

RECOMMENDED READING lists are long. Try *Delhi and Agra, A Travellers' Companion,* by Michael Alexander for a flavor of life in these two cities through the centuries. *Freedom at Midnight*

by Larry Collins and Dominque La Pierre is a fast-moving and highly-readable account of Indian independence; *Midnight's Children* won Indian author Salman Rushdie a Booker Prize and is considered one of the best English language books written about India. *Train to Pakistan* by Khushwant Singh is a moving account of the 1947 partition of India and Pakistan. *India, A Wounded Civilization*, by V.S. Naipaul is a controversial but interesting essay on the Indian mind. One of the best books written about the Mughals is Bamber Gascoigne's *The Great Moghuls*, which combines scholastic research with a simple, compelling style. Besides these are the classics such as *An Indian Summer* by James Cameron and Rudyard Kipling's *Plain Tales from the Hills*.

AGRA

THE MOODS OF THE TAJ MAHAL are best experienced during sunrise, sunset and on moonlit nights. Unfortunately, most day tours of Agra arrive at midday when the sun is at its harshest and the crowds at their largest. If you are staying for a while, try going at least twice — at 6:15 a.m. and 6:30 p.m. — when the Taj Mahal turns grey, pink and orange depending on the sunlight. During those hours this magnificent monument is truly stunning and most photogenic, but bring a tripod.
THE BEST WAY OF SEEING THE CITY is to hire an open-air, cycle rickshaw, so you can sightsee in a leisurely manner. The rates are Rs. 1.5 per kilometer and about Rs. 10 per hour. Ask for Lal Khan at the Taj View Agra. He is a remarkably fit and chatty rickshaw puller in his 50s.
BAZAARS worth exploring include several west of Agra fort, where one whole street is devoted to kite-making. The main attraction is Kinari Bazaar. It winds for about two kilometers northwest from the fort.
MARBLE PIETRA DURA, the non-porous marble from Makrana in Rajasthan (from which the Taj Mahal was built), is turned into table tops, cigarette boxes, plates and vases inlaid with semi-precious stones by thousands of craftsmen. They are descendants of the artisans hired by Shah Jahan and have in fact improved on the work of their forefathers. Get it throughout the city.
SUBHASH EMPORIUM, 18/1 Gwalior Rd., has the finest range of marble artifacts in Agra and arguably the best in India. Some of the 500 artisans

working for this emporium have won national awards for their work which is on display, but not for sale. Table tops intricately inlaid with semi-precious stones costing up to U.S.$15,000 are the best bet here. All items can be packed and shipped with insurance. Oswal Emporium, 30 Munro Road, also has a wide range.
KOHINOOR JEWELLERS, 41 MG Rd., is the best and most reliable shop in Agra. Quality is assured. It specializes in emeralds, mostly from India and Zambia, but cut here. The owner, Ghansyam Mathur, will give reliable advice. Munshi Ganeshi Lal and Sons has shops in Mahatma Gandhi Road and Fatehabad Road and is also reliable.
GOOD BUYS IN CARPETS AND DHURRIES can be found at Mangalik & Company, 5 Taj Rd., Sadar Bazàar. It also has a range of woolen carpets and dhurries made in villages around Agra including Kashmiri silk-cotton-wool carpets of various sizes from .45 x .3 m to 3.6 x 2.7 m. They can be made to order. Shipping and full insurance at reasonable rates.
BOOK SELECTION is best at the Modern Book Depot in the Sardar area on Taj Road.
RESTAURANTS WITH A WIDE RANGE of Indian, Continental, and Chinese cuisine can be found at all the top hotels in the city. The buffets at the Mughal Sheraton, Clarks Shiraz and Taj View are recommended. A la carte in these three varies, but Indian food in these restaurants are good. Besides top hotels, many good restaurants are also to be found in the Sardar area: Kwality Restaurant is a clean, two-story restaurant which offers vegetarian and non-vegetarian Indian, Continental and Chinese food. Recommended dishes include mutton *Barra Kebab*, Chinese soups and spring rolls and their Swiss-style confectionery; Prakash Restaurant serves up vegetarian fare while Laxmi Vilas gives good value for south Indian vegetarian food. Brijbasi Sweets and Restaurant has an excellent range of traditional Indian sweets, and in particular, Agra specialties.

Also try Capri Restaurant at Nari Parbat (Indian and Continental) and Sonam Restaurant at 51 Taj Rd., a former residence of a British army officer converted into a restaurant. The setting is simple; there are a few chairs under a giant chandelier, which appears out of place. But the food, especially the Indian and Mughlai fare, is excellent.

Travel Notes

Land and People

The capital of India comprises Old Delhi, built by the Mughal rulers, and New Delhi, built by the British. The city lies west of the Yamuna river. The Union Territory of New Delhi and its suburbs cover 1,489 square kilometers. It has a population of 7.8 million by 1988 estimates. It lies in north India's Indo-Gangetic plain and is sandwiched between the states of Uttar Pradesh and Haryana.

Agra, home of the Taj Mahal, is 203 kilometers south of Delhi. It bears the strong imprint of Mughal rulers who turned it into a city of monuments. Agra is one of the key cities of Uttar Pradesh. It measures 62 square kilometers and has a population of about 800,000.

Traveling in India can be a pleasure or a pain, depending on how well you prepare yourself. Nothing must be taken for granted in a country that apparently has mastered the art of bureaucracy, but in which a plethora of regulations can sometimes be miraculously cut through to accommodate the visitor.

Make all travel arrangements in advance, especially during the peak period (October-March), double-check bookings, preferably have them confirmed in writing, and make sure you have all necessary documents with you when traveling around India. Above all, be patient. Somehow things will sort themselves out in India as they have for millenia.

How to Get There

By Air

More than 20 international airlines and two domestic carriers — Indian Airlines and the feeder service, Vayudoot — operate flights to New Delhi. Agra is connected with Delhi, Khajuraho and Varanasi by daily flights and to Bombay and Jaipur everyday except Monday.

By Rail

India has the world's largest rail network and Delhi is the country's best-connected railhead. It is also the headquarters of the Northern Railways. There are two major stations — (Old) Delhi Main and New Delhi (passengers should first check which station they should go to) — and a number of other stations such as Nizamuddin, Sarai Rohilla and Delhi Cantonment. Bombay and Calcutta are linked to Delhi by the vestibuled and aircondi-

tioned Rajdhani Express with meals inclusive of the ticket cost on these two services.

The main classes of services are: Airconditioned First Class, Airconditioned Chair Car, Airconditioned 2nd Class Sleeper, Ordinary First Class and 2nd Class Sleepers. Meter-gauge trains do not have airconditioning. First Class train travel is generally cheaper than domestic flights.

There are numerous train services to and from Agra to various cities. One of the more popular services is the Taj Express which leaves Delhi at 7 a.m. daily and returns from Agra at 7 p.m. It is popular with tourists making day tours from Delhi. (Be extremely careful with personal belongings while boarding and while riding trains. There have been numerous cases of theft on trains between Delhi and Agra.)

By Road

Numerous buses ply to and from the Inter-state Bus Terminus near Kashmere Gate in Old Delhi. The city is at the intersection of several national highways and drivers are advised to first check out their road conditions. There have been reports of villagers damaging the cars of foreigners along the Delhi-Agra road.

Agra is well-connected by bus to major cities and tourist sites in the region. For inter-state services, go to Uttar Pradesh Road Transport Bus Stand at Idgah. It is open from 6 a.m. to 10 p.m. (Tel. 64198) or opposite Power House (74141).

Entry and Customs Rules

All foreigners except Nepalese, Bhutanese or South Africans of Indian origin require visas for entry into the country. The Indian government issues three kinds of visas for a fee of about US$5: 1) tourist visas are effective for three months and tourists must arrive within six months of the visa issue date; 2) entry visas are issued to persons visiting the country for business, employment or permanent residence; 3) transit visas are granted for those passing through India en route to another destination, on production of tickets for the onward journey. Maximum stay for transit visas is 15 days. Application to extend visas may be done at the Foreigners' Regional Registration Office (FRRO) at major cities. In New Delhi, go to the 1st Floor, Hans Bhavan, near the Tilak Bridge Railway Station (Tel. 272790).

Special permits are needed for foreigners intend-

ing to visit the following states or places: Punjab State, Darjeeling, Assam and Meghalaya, Andaman and Nicobar Islands and Sikkim. Permission and requests are to be directed to the Home Ministry.

A Foreign Travel Tax of Rs 300 is levied on passengers leaving for any destination outside India. For journeys to Afghanistan, Bangladesh, Bhutan, Burma, Nepal, Pakistan, Sri Lanka and the Maldives — Rs 50.

Foreigners can bring any amount of foreign currency or travelers' checks into India provided they declare the amount or checks on arrival in the Currency Declaration Form. Cash, bank notes and travelers' checks up to US$1,000 need not be declared at the time of entry. No Indian currency whatsoever, with the exception of rupee travelers' checks , can be taken in or out of India.

Prohibited articles include the import of gold, gold coins and gold and silver bullion — and the Indian government imposes strict regulations to check this — dangerous drugs and live plants. The export of antiquities more than 100 years old from India is banned. So is the export of wildlife, animal skins and articles made from them.

Visitors can bring in a bottle of liquor up to .95 liters and 200 cigarettes or 50 cigars or 250 grams of tobacco.

Income tax clearance certificates are required at the time of departure for foreigners who have stayed more than 90 days. Contact Foreign Section, Central Reserve Building, Indraprastha Estate (331-5807).

Medical Requirements

No vaccination is required for entry into India. But a valid certificate of vaccination for those coming from yellow fever-infected areas (mostly South and Central America, or Africa) is required. All foreigners, except diplomats and foreign journalists, intending to stay in India are required to undergo a compulsory Aids test but up to the time of printing this has not really been enforced except for foreign students. Visitors are advised to take vaccinations against typhoid, cholera, tetanus and hepatitis.

When to Go

The best time to visit Delhi and Agra is October to March. The climate of the two cities is similar. The rainy season is from June through September.

Temperatures range from sweltering highs of 46°C to pleasant lows of 22°C in summer. In winter, temperatures vary from 34°C to 4°C.

What to Wear

Light T-shirts, loose cottons and sneakers or sandals are the only things that will get you through a summer day. Bring along sunglasses or a wide-brimmed hat to protect your eyes — and brain — from the sun. Light woolens or a jacket will be needed during the winter, particularly at night.

Remember to remove your shoes before entering a place of worship or mausoleum. At mosques, heads must be covered and shorts are not allowed. At Jain temples, items made of leather, including bags and belts, are forbidden.

A-Z General Information on Delhi and Agra

Airport Information

Indira Gandhi International Airport has improved considerably in recent years, but delays in baggage collection for up to two hours are still common. The airport lies 17 kilometers southwest of the city center and has an international and domestic terminal. It is advisable to use the prepaid taxi or bus service to get into the city center. There are also porters and a small Rs 5 tip per trolley of luggage is ample. Passengers departing New Delhi on domestic flights should first check if their flights are for the Boeing or Airbus; there are different boarding points for these planes.

Bargaining

A growing number of shops are offering fixed price goods. Elsewhere, a discount of 5 to 15 per cent can be expected in curio and carpet shops, and more in bazaars. Practice the ancient eastern art of bargaining, especially for services, even for taxis in places where meters are not usually used. Go to recommended shops to ensure quality and a fair price. Bear in mind that any taxi driver or tour guide who brings you to a shop gets a commission of about ten per cent from the owners.

Bazaars

Bazaars in Agra are popular for shopping and meals. They are generally open from 10 a.m. to 8 p.m. but many stores and vendors stay open longer. Sardar Bazaar is closed on Tuesdays; other bazaars close on Mondays or Sundays.

Begging

Do not be deceived that beggars in large Indian cities are poor lonely souls desperate for their next meal. They may well be so but chances are that the beggar you meet is part of a larger, organized syndicate in which their chiefs get the lion's share of a day's takings. If you feel sufficiently moved to help the deprived masses, there are numerous charitable organizations in the country to which you can make donations.

Business Hours

Offices and shops are generally open from 10 a.m. to 5 p.m. everyday except Sundays. Banks function between 10 a.m. and 2 p.m. on Mondays to Fridays and 10 a.m. to noon on Saturdays.

Communications

India's phone and telex services are notoriously bad despite the fact that the government has launched several satellites into space. Most hotels should be able to book an international call, but it can take 30 minutes to get through. And even then the lines may not be clear. Calls may also be made if you go to the Central Telegraph Office at Eastern Court, along Jan Path, or the Overseas Communication Service office on Bangla Sahib Road.

In Agra, the Head Post Offices (open 10 a.m. to 5 p.m.) are at The Mall (Tel. 74000) and opposite Power House. The Central Telegraph Office (open 24 hours) is at The Mall (76914).

Electricity

The electrical current used in India is 220/250 volts and 50 cycles, alternating current.

Emergencies

Some useful telephone numbers:

Delhi

Police	100
Fire Brigade	101
Ambulance	102
Directory Enquiry	197
Telephone Assistance	199
Railway Enquiries	3317575
Railway Reservations	344877

The All India Institute of Medical Sciences (AIIMS) at Ansari Nagar (661123) and Ram Manohar Lohia Hospital at Babra Kharak Singh Marg (345525) are reputable hospitals.

Agra

Police	100, or 74444
Fire Brigade	101
Ambulance	102

Reliable hospitals are the District Hospital in M.G. Road (74236); Lady Lyall Hospital, Noori Gate Road (74184).

Guide Services

May be obtained outside the Taj Mahal. Rates are as follows:

	1-4 persons	5-15 persons	16-40 persons
Half day	Rs 48	Rs 60	Rs 80
Full day	Rs 72	Rs 85	Rs 95

(Lunch, outstation allowances and tips are extra)

Health and Medical Care

Be careful. The infamous Delhi Belly has conquered even the strongest stomach, so exercise caution. Drinking water should be boiled or at the very least properly filtered, but with the exception of top hotels this is not done. Those with weak stomachs should stick to mineral water, bottled drinks, coffee, tea, beer or wine during meals. If you can't take spicy food, ask the waiter for dishes which are milder, or cut down on spices and chillies. Avoid salads except in top hotels and recommended restaurants and take fruit which has skin that can be peeled off. Bring your own medical kit and make sure it has pills to help you fight diarrhea and stomach cramps. With the Aids scare, make sure it also has a few disposable syringes; they are hard to find in India. Be careful of dogs and monkeys because rabies is quite widespread in India.

Hotels

Since the 1982 Asian Games, the Non-Aligned Summit and Commonwealth Heads of Government Meeting in 1983, a number of top class hotels have been built in Delhi. Most of the top hotels in Agra have rooms overlooking the Taj Mahal. Make sure you ask for one, especially on moonlit nights.

Delhi

Expensive (Rs 1,000 per night and up):
— Hyatt Regency, Bhikaji Cama Place (Tel. 609911/Tlx. 031-61512).
— Le Meridien, Windsor Place (383960).

— Maurya Sheraton, Diplomatic Enclave (3010101/Tlx. 031-61447).
— Oberoi Intercontinental, Dr Zakir Hussain Marg (363030/Tlx. 031-3829).
— Taj Mahal, 1 Man Singh Rd. (3016162/Tlx. 031-66874).
— Taj Palace, 2 Sadar Patel Marg (3010404/Tlx. 031-62761).

Moderate (Rs 600-900):
— Claridges, 12 Aurangzeb Rd. (3010211/ Tlx. 031-62898).
— Kanishka, 19 Ashok Rd. (343400/Tlx.031-62788).
— Imperial, Jan Path (311511/ Tlx. 031-62603).
— Oberoi Maidens, 7 Sham Nath Marg (2525464/ Tlx.031-66801).

Agra

Expensive (Rs 800 and up):
— Clarks Shiraz, 5 Taj Rd. (72421/ Tlx. 0565-211).
— Taj View Agra, Fatehabad Road, Taj Ganj (64171/ Tlx. 0565-202)
— Welcomgroup Mughal Sheraton, Fatehabad Road, (64701/Tlx. 64704).
— Agra Ashok, The Mall (76223)

Moderate (Rs 200-400):
— Mumtaz Hotel, 181/2 Fatehabad Rd. (64771/ Tlx. 0565-222).
— Amar Hotel, Fatehabad Rd., (65696/Tlx. 0565-341).
— Grand Hotel, 137 Station Rd. (74014)

Language
English, Hindi, Punjabi and Urdu are widely spoken in Delhi and Agra.

Local Transport and Driving
Self-drive cars are not available in India. Those wishing to bring in their own cars must obtain a Customs Carnet and an International Certificate for Motor Vehicles (ICMV) from an automobile association or club in their own country. International Driving permits are not valid in India unless they are endorsed and countersigned by the Licensing Authority of the region in India.

Traffic in India moves on the left side of the road, another legacy of the Raj. The main modes of transport within the cities are public buses (not recommended), taxis and autorickshaws. Hire cars and limousines only from approved operators.

Taxis and autorickshaws are easily recognized by their yellow tops and black bodies. In Delhi, rates are fixed according to the meter but not in Agra. Seating capacity is five passengers for taxis and three for autorickshaws, also known as "three-wheelers."

The fares for both taxis and autorickshaws were increased in January 1988. The new flagdown charge for taxis is Rs 3.50 for the first 1.6 kilometers and Rs 2 per subsequent kilometer. There is a 25 per cent night charge between 11 p.m. and 5 a.m. Some meters for new rates have not yet been adjusted. Until they are, passengers have to pay 10 per cent more than the stated fare. A 50 paise charge is levied for each piece of luggage.

Tourist taxis can be hired from most leading hotels. The rate is Rs 2 per kilometer for non-airconditioned cars (Rs 4 for airconditioned cars) and a detention charge of Rs 15 per hour. Coaches approved by the Government of India can be hired from the Delhi Tourism Development Corporation, N-36, Middle Circus, Connaught Circus (Tel. 3313637). The public bus service is operated by the Delhi Transport Corporation which, unfortunately, is badly-run and strike-prone. Minimum fare is 50 paise. Recommended only for the adventurous or destitute. A list of approved car operators may be obtained from the Tourist Information Office.

In Agra, taxis are available at all railway stations at Rs 2.20 per kilometer. Rates for full-day hire are negotiable. Taxis from hotels are more expensive and the rates are often fixed. To hire transport for tours out of Agra, the rates are as follows:

Hours	Taxi	Deluxe	Deluxe
		Coach	Minibus
One	Rs 45	Rs 100	Rs 70
Four (Half day)	110	420	255
Ten (Full day)	320	1,265	700

Transport in Agra can be hired from Ashok Travels (Tel. 64171), Pleasure Tours (67462), Taj Travels (66576), Tour Aids India (73517), Travel Corporation of India (64111), Sita World Travels (64978), Travel Bureau (66118), UP State Tourism Development Corporation (72123).

Government buses also leave every 45 minutes from Idgah for Fatehpur Sikri (Rs 6 each way). No

buses go to Sikandra but taxis and autorickshaws may be hired to go there.

Cycle rickshaws and autorickshaws in Agra charge Rs 1.5 per kilometer. But for short distances there is a minimum fare of Rs 5. Cycle rickshaws provide a pleasant way of seeing the city, seated one or two to an open-air rickshaw: no noise, no petrol fumes, only "chappati power." Hire for an entire day costs Rs 75, but the average is Rs 10 per hour, and negotiable. Rickshaw pullers often say "As you like" when asked for a fare. That can lead to unpleasant scenes because they may often not like what you pay at the end. So insist on a fixed rate.

Some smaller hotels also offer bicycles for hire. You must place a deposit of money or your passport. Horse carriages are also available with negotiable rates.

Money Matters

The rupee is divided into 100 paise. Paper notes are circulated for the following denominations of rupee: 1, 2, 5, 10, 20, 100, 500. Coins are in denominations of 5, 10, 20, 25, and 50 paise. The exchange rate is roughly Rs 16 to US$1. (A black market thrives in most major cities and tourist towns, offering rates more than 10 per cent higher, but this is prohibited and there is a risk of getting counterfeit notes.) Money can be exchanged easily at banks at points of entry and hotels. Insist on a receipt when doing so and retain all receipts; without them, you cannot re-convert unspent rupees when you finally leave India. All foreign nationals have to pay their hotel bills and concessional tickets such as Discover India Fares in foreign currency, cash or travelers' checks. Rupees are accepted for payment of these only with proof of encashment in India of foreign currency. Credit cards (American Express, Diners Club, Visa and Master Card) are generally accepted by larger hotels, shops and tour agencies.

Photography

Bring your own camera and buy film before coming in, because it is more expensive in India. Each person is allowed to bring in five rolls but customs officials do not seem to be terribly strict if you bring in twice as much. There are no restrictions on taking pictures of most of India's monuments. But video and movie cameras are not permitted inside the compounds of the Taj Mahal. Still photography inside the main mausoleum of the Taj Mahal is also prohibited. You will find Indians generally willing to be photographed but snake charmers, street performers and musicians expect to be paid about Rs 10 if you want to take pictures of them.

Public Festivals and Holidays

The days of many festivals and holidays in India vary from year to year. Only the dates of fixed holidays are provided in the listing below.

January/February

Lohri — This festival marks the climax of the north Indian winter. In New Delhi, it is celebrated with the lighting of bonfires by children who go around singing and collecting money for firewood. In the middle of January, there is also a Rose Show and Flower Show in New Delhi.

Makara Sankranti — This Hindu festival is celebrated by a ritual dipping in rivers or seas (in the Yamuna river for Delhi and Agra) to mark the commencement of the sun's journey to the northern hemisphere.

Republic Day (Jan. 26, public holiday) — Amid much pomp and ceremony, New Delhi dons its finest on this day to commemorate the declaration of India as a republic on January 26, 1950. Tanks, missiles and India's latest military hardware roll along Raj Path towards India Gate, followed by caparisoned elephants and camels, colorful floats and Indian dancers. Folk dancing is also held in Delhi on January 27 and 28. This is a truly splendid festival. Don't miss it.

Beating the Retreat (Jan. 29) — This solemn and beautiful sunset pageant, which follows Republic Day, combines various sections of the armed forces in a parade that is, perhaps ironically, reminiscent of the British Raj. The Central Secretariat is festooned with lights while the camel regiment and cavalry stand on parade on the ramparts of the sandstone building, forming a magnificent silhouette with Rashtrapati Bhavan (the Presidential Palace) in the backdrop.

Vasant Panchami — This festival honors Saraswati, the Goddess of Wisdom and Learning, with worship conducted within the home with books, pens, paint brushes and musical instruments placed at the altar of the goddess.

Maha Shivaratri — The worship of Shiva, the third deity of the Hindu Trinity, is celebrated with believers chanting prayers all night and fairs near temples during the day.

Holi — The joyous festival heralding the advent

of spring — and the return of sunshine and color — is celebrated with the throwing of colored powder or water. On the night before, a bonfire is lit and a bamboo and straw effigy of the demoness Holika is set ablaze as people dance around the flames.

Delhi Horse Show — Show jumping and equestrian feats go on display during this show in mid-February.

March/April

Good Friday (public holiday) and Easter — As in the West, these Christian festivals, along with Christmas, are also observed in India.

Mahavir Jayanti (public holiday) — This festival commemorates the birth of Mahavira, the founder of Jainism, an ascetic religion which stresses non-violence.

Baisakhi — For Hindus, this festival marks the descent of the Ganges river to earth and devotees often dip themselves in rivers. Sikhs revere the religious importance of this day some 500 years ago when Guru Gobind Singh converted them into a martial race.

Buddha Jayanti (public holiday) — This is an important day of worship for Buddhists because it celebrates the birth, enlightenment and attainment of nirvana of Buddha.

Ram Navami — Devotees chant prayers and sing ballads to mark the birthday of the Hindu god Rama.

Id-ul Fitr (public holiday) — For Muslims, this day marks the end of their fasting month and also commemorates the descent of the Koran from heaven.

July/August

Bakrid (public holiday) — Muslims commemorate God's request of Hazrat Ibrahim to sacrifice his own son. Each family sacrifices one animal a day amid much feasting and rejoicing.

Raksha Bandhan — Hindu women tie decorative threads called *rakhi* on the wrists of their brothers to remind them of their duty to protect their sisters when the need arises.

Independence Day (public holiday) — August 15.

Janmashtami — Hindus celebrate the birth of Krishna with feasts and merriment after a fast. The childhood pranks of Krishna are reenacted in some parts of the country with young cowherds stealing pots of butter. But today young boys form human pyramids to reach out for gifts of money — rather

than butter — in the pots.

Sheetla Fair — Held in Agra near the Delhi Gate of the old fort.

August/September

Ganesh Chaturthi — Ganesh, the elephant-headed god is worshiped as the remover of obstacles.

Muharram (public holiday) — Shi'ite Muslims commemorate the death of their founders Hussein and Ali. Some Muslims in the Walled City of Old Delhi engage in self-flagellation by whipping themselves or cutting their skin with razors.

Kailash Fair — Held at Kailash Temple, 12 kilometers from Agra. It has become sanctified by the belief that Lord Shiva appeared there.

September/October

Dussehra (public holiday) — Also known as Navaratri or Durga Puja. This popular Indian festival lasts nine nights. It honors the goddesses Durga, Lakshmi and Saraswati. The tenth day, Dussehra, commemorates the victory of Rama, in the epic *Ramayana,* over Ravana, thus securing freedom for his captive wife, Sita. In Delhi and Agra, as in much of north India, the day is called Ram Lila. Crowds burn huge figures of the demon Ravana, his brother and son.

Mahatma Gandhi's birthday — (October 2, public holiday).

Sharad Purnima — This famous fair takes place at the Taj Mahal in Agra on the full moon night in October.

Phoowalon-ki-Sair — This is a festival in New Delhi in which Hindu and Muslim flower bearers carry palm fronds to be blessed at the Muslim shrine and Hindu temple in Mehrauli, near the Qutb Minar.

October/November

Diwali (public holiday) — Oil lamps are lit to show the god Rama the way home after 14 years of exile and to signify the triumph of good over evil. The festival is the most important one in the Hindu calendar and is also celebrated as Naraka Chaturdashi, when Lord Krishna destroyed the demon of darkness, Narakasura.

November/December

Gurpurab (public holiday) — Sikhs celebrate the birthday of their founder, Guru Nanak.

Chrysanthemum Show — This takes place at the Delhi YWCA, Ashoka Road.

Christmas (public holiday) — public holiday.

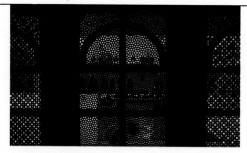

Taboos and Customs

Indians often will go out of their way to help you, but they tend not to be punctual. Be patient. Also, if invited to dinner by an Indian be prepared to take the first bite at around 10 p.m. after seemingly endless chatter and drinks. A small gift, such as a bunch of flowers and perhaps a bottle of liquor, would be appreciated by your host.

Hindus do not take beef, which is not sold legally in India, and Muslims shun pork. Many Hindus are also vegetarians, which is an important point to remember when dining with an Indian. Indians are generally friendly, even if they appear to be hopelessly curious about foreigners. Do not be surprised or offended if a stranger comes out of the blue, stares at you or strikes up a conversation as if you were a long-lost friend. Exercise caution by keeping an eye on your personal belongings at all times.

Time

Indian time is 5 1/2 hours ahead of Greenwich Mean Time and 9 1/2 hours ahead of American Eastern Standard Time.

Tourist Information Offices

The airport and all major train and bus stations have tourist information branches in Delhi. The main Government of India Tourist Office in the capital is at 88 Jan Path (320005/320342). The Delhi Tourism Development Corporation is located at N-Block, Connaught Circus (3313637/

3315322).

In Agra, there's a tourist office at 191 The Mall (72377), opposite the General Post Office. It is open from 9 a.m. to 5:30 p.m. from Mondays to Fridays, and from 9 a.m. to 1 p.m. on Saturdays. It is closed on all full national holidays. It is a useful place to get maps and basic information.

Tours

City tours in Delhi are conducted by the Delhi Tourism Development Corporation (DTDC) at N-36 Bombay Life Building, Connaught Place, Middle Circus (3313637) and the Indian Tourism Development Corporation (ITDC), L-Block, Connaught Circus (350331). Both provide half, full-day or evening tours. The ITDC tours are better, but cost slightly more (Rs 30 for half day and Rs 60 for a full day.)

Out-of-city tours are also conducted by ITDC and leading hotels. A day package to Agra costs about Rs 250 while overnight packages are about Rs 700. The Golden Triangle Tour of Delhi-Agra-Jaipur costs about Rs 1,500. Vayudoot Airline (699272) also offers seasonal tours around India.

Tours of the Taj Mahal, Agra Fort and Fatehpur Sikri are conducted by the UP State Tourism Development Corporation at Taj Khema, Eastern Gate, Taj Mahal (65383) and the UP State Road Transport Corporation, 96 Gwalior Rd. (72206). Full-day tours begin at 10.15 a.m. and end at 6.30 p.m. and cost about Rs 40, while half-day tours of Fatehpur Sikri cost Rs 30.

Useful Vocabulary

English	Hindi
Greetings	Namaste
Goodbye	Phir milenge
How are you?	Ap kaise hain?
How much?	Kitne paise
Too much	Bahut zyada hai
Good	Achha
Bad	Kharab
Please	Kripaya
Thank you	Shukrya
Yes	Har (nasalised)
No	Nahi
Water	Panni
Food	Khanna
Cold	Thanda
Hot	Garam
Doctor	Doctor

*A barebodied Indian mystic performs yoga in the blistering heat on the banks of the Yamuna River near the Taj Mahal (**above**). Islam has left an indelible mark on Agra. Two men take refuge from the 100-degree heat of the north Indian summer under the shadow of the Taj Mahal's main gate, which is embellished with motifs and inlay work of the Mughal builders (**preceding pages**).*

Index